Selina's Legacy

Selina's Legacy

A sequel to Selina of Sussex
1818-1886

Leonard Holder

Don't you see that children are GOD 's best gift?
the fruit of the womb his generous legacy?

Psalm 127:3 *

Library of Congress Control Number:		2020909507
ISBN:	Hardcover	978-1-9845-9491-4
	Softcover	978-1-9845-9490-7
	eBook	978-1-9845-9489-1

Scripture quotations marked KJV are from the Holy Bible, King James Version (Authorized Version). First published in 1611. Quoted from the KJV Classic Reference Bible, Copyright © 1983 by The Zondervan Corporation.

Any people depicted in stock imagery provided by Getty Images are models, and such images are being used for illustrative purposes only.
Certain stock imagery © Getty Images.

With illustrations by Cherrie Irwin

Print information available on the last page.

Rev. date: 05/30/2020

To order additional copies of this book, contact:
Xlibris
800-056-3182
www.Xlibrispublishing.co.uk
Orders@Xlibrispublishing.co.uk
810895

Contents

PART 1
My Childhood Limden Farm
1842 - 1856

PART 2
My teenage years at Perching Manor Farm
1856 – 1868

PART 3
Married life in Patcham
1868 -1885

PART 4
Widowhood
1885 -1921

I dedicate this book to Ruth's great-great-great-grandchildren: Barnaby, Sophia, Timothy, David, Beatrice, Benedict and John Holder. Their 21st century lives in Switzerland, couldn't be further removed from the life of their ancestor Ruth.

With many thanks to Cherrie Irwin for all her help in preparing this book for publication and for her artistic illustrations.

Family Tree
(Simplified)

Eli Page   -   Selina Westgate
b. 11 Oct 1817   *b. 17 Aug 1818*
Married 12 Feb 1838

|

Ruth Page   -   Dan Holder
b. 2 July 1841   *b. 9 Jan 1844*
Married 13 April 1868

|

Ebenezer Dan Holder   -   Mary Gertrude White
b. 3 April 1877   *b. 31 Dec 1883*
Married 13 Sept 1908

|

Edgar Ebenezer Holder   -   Ellen Rachel Wilkins
b. 15 July 1909   *b. 28 July 1908*
Married 16 Jan 1937

|

Leonard Edgar Holder   -   Phyllis Mary Pittwell
b. 3 April 1946   *b. 22 Nov 1946*
Married 3 June 1967

|

Geoffrey Leonard Holder   Daniel Francis Holder
b. 5 April 1968   *b. 5 May 1970*
and Ruth Anne Leyshon   *and* Martina Franz
Married 30 Dec 1995   *Married 12 Sept 1993*

| |

Barnaby John Holder   Sophia Evangeline Holder
b. 31 Oct 1997   *b. 23 Jan 1998*
Timothy Dyffdd Leonard Holder   David Gregory Holder
b. 12 Feb 1999   *b. 28 Jan 2000*
Beatrice Ellen Holder   Benedict Francis Holder
b. 13 July 2000   *b. 16 Oct 2001*

John Michael Holder
b. 2 Feb 2008

Author's Introduction

This book is a sequel to '*Selina of Sussex 1818-1886*' in which Selina, wife of Eli Page, farmer and Baptist minister, shares many aspects of her interesting and challenging life in rural Sussex, England, in the 19th century.

I gladly acknowledge that much in both of these books is imaginary. However Selina, her husband Eli, all her children and grandchildren and most of the other characters appearing in the books are true historical characters. The imaginary details of the narrative should be seen as flesh built upon the bare bones of fact. If I have strayed from the truth in my portrayal of these delightful characters, long since departed this life, it is to bring clarity rather than detract in any way from who they were and how they lived. Footnotes indicate the sources of my information.

My grandfather's grandmother was Selina Page and Ruth Holder was his mother. Both '*Selina of Sussex*' and this sequel '*Selina's Legacy*' are dedicated to my grandchildren with the prayer that both books will excite an interest, not only in rural Sussex with its history, from whence our family stems, but also the Christian faith which moulded and motivated their lives.

After Ruth's death, my grandfather Ebenezer Dan published an obituary to his mother in the Gospel Standard based on her own testimony. I have drawn on this considerably, meaning that most of the spiritual struggles and blessings recounted here are in no way fictional, but true to Ruth's own testimony.

Leonard Holder

Ruth's account of her mother's passing to glory*

My mother, Selina Page, née Westgate's influential life came to a close on Monday 8th February 1886. Having been born in August 1818 meant she was in her 68th year when God took her.

The doctor's writing on her death certificate is difficult to decipher but in layman's terms, it would appear that heart failure was the cause of death. This is not very informative, for as far as my thinking goes, everyone eventually dies of heart failure.

Over a period of some months, it was clear that Mum's health was deteriorating and during this time she battled with fears about her salvation and the reality of her faith in Christ. She was not one who could speak much to her family about spiritual things being very much under the shadow of my father, but about a month before she died it was wonderful to see how God was preparing her to leave this earthly life. A hymn which blessed her in those last days was one by Elliott and Toplady, number 471 in our Gadsby's Hymns:

Prepare me, gracious God,
To stand before thy face;
Thy Spirit must the work perform,
For it is all of grace.

---

* Edited by the author from details gleaned in an obituary of Selina Page by her daughter Ruth Holder, published in The Gospel Standard 1886

In Christ's obedience clothe,
And wash me in his blood;
So shall I lift my head with joy
Among the sons of God.

Do thou my sins subdue;
Thy sovereign love make known,
The spirit of my mind renew,
And save me in thy Son.

Let me attest thy power;
Let me thy goodness prove,
Till my full soul can hold no more
Of everlasting love.

During the last couple of weeks of her life I spent a lot of time at Perching Manor. On the last Tuesday morning of January, she appeared to be failing fast and so we called the doctor. He told us there was still hope of a recovery, but soon after, Mum deteriorated. Her faith, however, at this point, came to the fore and she commented in a low voice:

'I'm not looking to the doctor to cure me and I'm not looking to the prayers of your father to save me.'

'No, it's only Jesus who can do us good,' I answered, understanding exactly what she was saying.

Mum's face lit up and with a wonderful smile she nodded in agreement.

For several days after this she was unconscious. On the Friday she knew us and although she tried to speak, her voice seemed to be paralysed. Sensing that she looked at peace but wanted to tell us something I said,

'Darling Mother, do you want to tell us what a dear Saviour you have found?'

Mum's responding smile showed clearly that this was so.

'Do you want me to tell all your dear children that having Jesus by faith is sufficient to die with?' I continued.

Once again her answering smile clearly showed her agreement.

Within the space of a week, we could see she was sinking fast, but on the Saturday she seemed to recognise us again. On Sunday morning I said, 'I am going to chapel now Mother.'

'Please pray for me constantly,' she managed to reply.

She spoke to each one who came to see her, but her voice became so weak, that sadly, most of the time we really couldn't understand what she was trying to say.

About two hours before she died, she revived a little, her face brightened and she said, 'I am going to heaven. I shall see the Saviour.'

She lay quietly for about an hour, and then, without a struggle or a groan, gently breathed her last. Thus died one of the best of parents, and we are but left to mourn her loss.

Ruth's Preface

Picking up the baton

We all missed Mum terribly but accepted that God had given her a good life, protected her through the births of fourteen babies, given her much wisdom both in her relationship with Dad and also in bringing us children up to be God-fearing citizens. Now, however, we had to take up the baton and continue the race without her.

Shortly before she died, Mum showed me the account she had written of her life which astonished me considerably. She explained that it wasn't always easy to share her deepest thoughts in conversation either with Eli, her husband, or with her children, and she hoped recording things in writing might be an effective way of influencing the following generations.

'God is very real to me,' she said. 'I can't preach like father, but I long that all my children, my grandchildren, and in time their children and grandchildren, might all experience the same happiness I have found through my faith in Jesus. I can leave this life with full confidence of an ongoing and far closer relationship with the Son of God throughout eternity and am praying that we will all be there, wherever 'there' is, to share it together.'

Mum also added that so much had changed during her lifetime and as even greater changes seemed to be on the way, she wanted to share with future generations how life had been for her and her family in rural Sussex in the nineteenth century.

'Ruth,' she said, 'maybe you can find it in you to continue the story?'

'Oh, Mum,' I gasped, 'I don't think so.'

'Don't think about whether you can or can't,' Mum answered. 'Just begin to do it. Aim to do it for the glory of God and I'm sure he will help you.'

I realised later, as I thought about Mum's words, that they succinctly expressed the secret of her own fruitful life.

Therefore with trepidation, I'm taking on the task and I pray that my story will be a worthy successor to Mum's inspiring biography. I must acknowledge that reading what my mother had written impressed me. It revealed her to me in a new and wonderful light. She had always lived in the shadow of my very dominant father and as children we had very rarely considered her thoughts and feelings. She was just mother, the dependable anchor in our young lives. Now with a husband and children of my own, I am finding it extremely encouraging and challenging to learn the secret of the confidence and peace which she exuded, making her the wonderful woman we were proud to call our mother.

Reading recently in my Bible, from the Epistle to the Hebrews:

By faith Abel offered unto God a more excellent sacrifice than Cain, by which he obtained witness that he was righteous, God testifying of his gifts: and by it he being dead yet speaketh.[2]

I felt very much the sentiments of this verse could apply equally to my mother and her writings.

---

[2] Hebrews 11:4

Part 1

My Childhood
Limden Farm
1842 - 1856

Chapter 1

Early Memories

I f I'd had the opportunity to choose my own name I couldn't have chosen a better one. Apart from my older brother Richard, who is named after my father's father, all of Mum and Dad's children have biblical names. It could of course be argued that Mercy is another exemption, but mercy is a strong biblical concept. Anyway, I really love the Old Testament character of Ruth, after whom I was named.

Although the biblical Ruth was originally a Moabite, with an upbringing steeped in a heathen culture, she ended up marrying into a Jewish family. After being widowed, Ruth accompanied her mother-in-law back to Israel with those famous words of faith and allegiance on her lips: *'Thy people shall be my people and thy God my God.'* [1] It's strange but whilst reading my mother's story I felt those same words re-echoing in my own heart.

Soon after the death of my grandfather Richard Page and before either of them reached twenty-one, my mother Selina Westgate and my father Eli Page were married. Their first home was Clifton Farm, Arlington, which is now part of Upper Dicker in East Sussex. This is where I was born on July 2nd 1841, the third child in the family and the first daughter. Early in 1842, before my first birthday, we

---

[1] Ruth.1:16

moved further north in Sussex to Limden Farm, Ticehurst, so I have no recollection of Clifton Farm at all. Limden Farm is where all my childhood memories are held.

Limden Farmhouse

These memories for the most part are extraordinarily happy ones. A well run farmhouse is a very healthy environment for children, far more so than the blacksmith's shop where I am bringing up my own family. Mum had two girls helping her in the house and dairy, one of whom for a period of time, was my cousin Sarah Westgate and then later another cousin Ruth Parris. My two older brothers and I were also given jobs to do, those suitable for our age and ability. I loved feeding the hens with Mum and one of my earliest jobs was collecting the eggs from the laying boxes in the henhouse. I had a little basket lined with hay and Mum showed me how to very carefully collect the eggs and then bring to her so that she could transfer them to a larger basket. Thinking back now, I'm sure Mum

Basket of eggs

could have done the job far quicker without me, but I realise that she saw my participation as an important part of my education. Later of course I could do it all by myself.

Richard and John, my two older brothers, also had their jobs to do. Richard is nearly three years older than me and John, who was born in February 1840, is my senior by just over a year. They were given more manly jobs. For example, they were made responsible to ensure there was always a supply of wood by the kitchen fire. This meant bringing it in from the shed in the yard outside the back door, which we called the outhouse. I also remember that Richard, as quite a young boy, used to feed the pigs. Most of the milk from our cows was turned into butter but the skimmed milk which was left after scooping the thicker cream from the top of the setting dishes, was an important part of the pigs' diet. It had to be carried across the yard to the pig sty and tipped into their feeding troughs. As the boys got older Dad gave them increasingly more jobs to do on the farm. I never heard them complain. Work was part of living and we were each well aware that some children had it far harder than we did. For instance, there were the little boys who worked for our chimney sweep and had to climb up inside our chimney to sweep it. I remember Richard once saying what fun this would be, but he changed his tune when one poor urchin emerged spluttering and coughing, enveloped in soot from head to toe.

Another regular job the boys eventually took over was that of emptying the toilet buckets. The toilet was in a small, unassuming shed outside and was composed of a wooden seat with two different sized holes suitable for a variety of shapes and sizes of bottoms. The buckets below the seat needed emptying each day. Dad would ensure there was a trench dug in a nearby field ready for this human waste, as for some reason he didn't allow it to be thrown on the animal manure heap. A new trench was dug every week or so.

I also had a younger brother, Samuel, born at the end of Mum and Dad's first year at Limden Farm. Samuel was named after Mum's father who had died earlier that year. I think I can say that as we grew up, Samuel was my best friend. The older boys had each other but because Samuel was younger than me, Mum expected me to look after him and this gave us a special bond. Later I was to have a string of younger sisters, the closest to me in age being Orpah, born in 1844, then Naomi, born in 1846, but still, I always related better to Samuel.

It's only since I've had a husband and children of my own that I have thought back in admiration at the way Mum managed things in my early childhood. She was still young herself, only twenty-two when I, her third child was born. Also thinking back, I realise that Dad wasn't the easiest of husbands, although I know they were devoted to each other. An important part of each day was our family prayer time and Mum's faith and trust in God were clear to all who knew her. She would pray with us and for us when Dad was away. I well remember her regularly asking God for help and wisdom to run her home and family in a way that glorified him.

My father Eli was a Baptist minister as well as being a full time farmer so even when I was young, he would often be away preaching on Sundays. However, whether Dad was with us or not, each Sunday Mum would dress us in our best clothes and we would drive all the way down to the little chapel at Burwash in our pony and trap. We children enjoyed Sundays, firstly because we didn't have jobs to do and secondly because of the outing itself to Burwash. The ride was fun and we always particularly looked forward to going through the toll gate at Stonegate. The man there knew Mum and Dad and because we were going to a church service, we were allowed through the gate without charge. However he generally liked to have a little chat so it was no good hurrying him because we had to wait for him to open the gate.

It was only as I got older that I began to really understand anything that was said by the preacher in the Sunday service, but I used to enjoy the experience of chapel and liked to sing along with some of the hymns as I got to know them.

I'd like to tell you about our farm. The postal address of Limden Farm is Ticehurst, despite the fact that the closest village is actually Stonegate. The latter is where we children went to school, but more about that later. Running north from Stonegate, to join the Ticehurst to Wadhurst road, is Limden Lane. It's a narrow, densely-wooded lane, bordered as you leave Stonegate by large deciduous trees, mainly oak, which in many places overhang the road making it quite dark and creepy. After a bit, the lane drops steeply down Mabbs Hill, at the bottom of which, to the right-hand side, lay Limden Farm.

It is years since I visited it, but that lane leading from Stonegate to my childhood home, holds so many memories. Our little river which ran from the north parallel to Limden Lane, couldn't continue further south as the land rises, so it made an abrupt ninety degree turn eastwards under the lane and then flowed close to our farmhouse and on eastward across our fields. I know Mum was always nervous about the river because although it wasn't deep, she knew that if, as small children, we fell in, we could easily drown. Thankfully none of us ever did fall in and in reality it was a pretty safe river. It was slow flowing resulting in the accumulation of silt along its edge which over the years had provided a muddy base for reeds and grasses to grow. There were a few places where the water came right to the bank, good places from which to fish, but in general the reeds provided a natural barrier to stop little children falling in.

I'm sure if I went back again now those childhood haunts would seem so much smaller than I remember them as a child, but we got to know nearly every square inch of our farm with its sprawling fields and familiar woods.

We farmed ninety-five acres. I say 'we' because although Dad was employing five regular farm workers he always ensured that we children did our bit too. Haymaking was a favourite time. The men would mow the grass with scythes and we children would then help to turn the hay so that thorough exposure ensured proper drying. Once completely dry, it was loaded onto a cart. Our lovely old cart-horse, Big-foot, would bring it nearer the house and barns where the men would build a haystack. I remember Dad saying that the haystack must be near the animal sheds, where it would be needed in winter, but far enough away so that if it caught fire neither building nor animals would be in danger. The top of the haystack was always thatched, as this helped to keep the rain out, and thatching was a job Dad always did himself in my early days.

We children loved to help build the haystack. As the hay was brought from the fields and the haystack was slowly built up, it was our job to jump about on the glorious, soft, dried grass to help squash it down. On a warm summer's day the hay had such a deliciously,

distinctive smell that even now, when I smell cut grass drying in the fields, I get quite nostalgic about those happy, childhood days. One year Richard and John built a den in the haystack. The stack had been finished and thatched and working around the back where they couldn't be seen from the house, they pulled out clumps of hay and made a short passageway into a larger cavity deep

Haystack

within the haystack. They then stuffed hay back into the entrance to hide the way in. Sometimes they allowed Samuel and me to play in there too. It was our secret place and great fun. But then Dad discovered it. He was livid. After explaining to the boys the danger of getting inside the haystack - apparently the hay could collapse on top of them and suffocate them to death, he delivered a good hiding to ensure they understood what dreadful danger they'd been in and dissuade them from ever doing it again.

Chapter 2

Childhood Fears

Looking back now, the memory of those days seems idyllic. Although as children we had none of the major responsibilities which come through adulthood and marriage, I do remember worries and fears which would often keep me awake at night. The one which seemed to loom the largest, was an awful fear of dying. I knew several families where children my age had died and we had lost our own little brother Eb soon after his first birthday and just before my eighth in 1849. Eb's death really upset me. For days I would cry myself to sleep at night and then after a while I began to dread the possibility of my own death.

Ebenezer's gravestone

At first this fear of death was linked with the fact that we had sealed baby Eb in a little box and buried him in the graveyard at Stonegate. I found it inconceivable to reconcile this with the Eb I knew and loved - a living little boy. He had laughed and cried, smiled and played with me and now he was lying underground with the worms. All of this haunted me, and I was terrified.

Mum and Dad talked to us about Eb's death but it was some days before what they said truly sank in. I was too upset about losing little Eb to think further than this. Later I could be comforted by Mum and Dad's assurance that it was only Eb's body that we had buried. Eb himself wouldn't be worrying as he was with Jesus in heaven. Dad explained in a way that we children could understand how heaven is a holy place where everything is good and true. It's God's home and he doesn't allow anything or anyone who is not good and true to be there. Goodness and truth bring happiness so the complete goodness and truth in heaven bring complete happiness. He explained that no one is good enough for heaven and that only Jesus can make us worthy to go there.

I thought a lot about this happiness because so much of the time I knew I was not really happy. *'What sort of things made me unhappy?'* I asked myself.

To begin with, I blamed other people. Sometimes Richard and John teased and laughed at me, sometimes to the point of tears. I remember so vividly the afternoon we had been coming home from school, when suddenly the boys had run off and left me alone. I had tried to be brave as I walked down the lane by myself. The rascals jumped out at me from behind a tree and scared the living daylights out of me. *'Yes,'* I reasoned, *'that was not kind and good; in heaven that will never happen.'*

Then there was the time that Dad had punished me. Mum had been very angry about something I had done and when she told father he had taken me outside and given me a hard smacking. *'That was not kind and good,'* I thought to myself. Then I realised that I was the one who was not good. I knew if I was honest with myself, that I had deserved that smacking.

I think it was at that point, it started to dawn on me that so much of my unhappiness had its source within my own being. If I didn't get what I wanted, I became miserable and irritable, causing me to say and do unkind things to others. This would then start a downward spiral of unhappiness both for me and often the rest of the family too.

As I look back now, I can see these thoughts were probably the beginning of what father would call 'God's grace' working in me. I needed to be convinced that I was a sinner before I would want to trust Jesus as my Saviour. This realisation of my own sin was God graciously leading me to himself. However, it was many years later before I found the peace of knowing my sins were forgiven.

My sinfulness began to frighten me. I tried so hard to be good but mostly it didn't work. I'd find all sorts of unbidden thoughts coming into my mind especially when things didn't go my way, resulting in more bitterness and anger. It was only later, sometimes much later that I was penitent for the way I had reacted and regretted the things I had thought and said.

I had no doubt about the existence of the God of the Bible. We listened to his word every day, talked to him in family prayers and I had been taught to kneel at my bedside and say my own personal prayers to him before going to sleep each night. I would always ask him to forgive my sins, but when I perpetually kept thinking and doing sinful things, I was sure he couldn't keep forgiving me. I also had the shocking realisation that a part of me loved those sins and even enjoyed being unkind, getting my own back and doing forbidden things. Such a revelation frightened me even more and I began to think about hell and the eternal punishment the Bible warns us about.

There were nights when I was simply petrified about going to bed. I was sure that if I died in the night I would wake up in hell. Sometimes, I would cry myself to sleep in utter despair and be overwhelmingly relieved when I woke up in the morning, finding myself in my own bed with the birds still singing happily outside the window.

What compounded my problem was the fact that I couldn't talk to anyone about my innermost struggles. Usually after a few days or as long as maybe a week, I'd find I could manage to stifle my conscience and convince myself that I didn't really care about these 'foolish thoughts' as I described them. It could be months before they came back to plague me again, but rest assured, come back they always did.

I did have other less troublesome fears, but from what I could gather from my childhood companions, such fears were common amongst many Sussex children at that time. Our family's faith in God was no doubt the reason for such fears not having a prominent place in my young heart and mind. We were brought up to believe that the God of the Bible whom we could address as our Father in heaven, was in control of everything and that there was no such thing as mere chance or luck. Therefore we laughed rather at the superstitious notion of bad luck resulting from spying a single magpie or if a black cat ran across our path. On an aside, I have to admit that thunderstorms terrified me no end.

Chapter 3

School and Clothes

When I was about five years old I started school. My two older brothers were already going down the lane to the National School in Stonegate five days a week, so in one way I had been quite looking forward to being grown up enough to join them. However, I must say it was nevertheless a daunting enough prospect leaving the security of our family home and facing new experiences.

The school was linked to the Anglican church in Stonegate so each school day started and ended with prayers. For me this wasn't a strange thing as worshipping and talking to God was such an integral part of our family life, however using a prayer book was not. At home Dad would simply talk to God and although he had some phrases he often repeated, he never read a prayer from any book. This was also the way we learned to say our own prayers as we knelt by our beds each night. My prayer might be the same, or nearly the same each night but I always felt it to be very personal, not one written by someone else. In addition, I already knew most of the Bible stories taught and remember being very shocked that some of the other children knew incredibly little about the Bible and more so, spoke and behaved in ways I'd never witnessed before.

Our teacher a Miss Mary Read, taught us what was often referred to as the three R's: reading, writing and arithmetic, and either the vicar or someone else from the church would teach us Scripture and the catechism. Because school was not compulsory not all parents insisted their children attend every day; I'm sure this must have complicated things somewhat for Miss Read. As much as possible, we were divided into two groups. If one group was having a lesson with the vicar or his representative, then the other had Miss Read for one of her lessons. A lot of the time however, we were all together and Miss Read would often ask the older children to assist the younger ones. She soon deduced which of her older pupils were the best 'teachers'. In those days, we were only expected to have four, or at the very most, five years of schooling, so the oldest child in the school would hardly have reached his or her eleventh birthday.

I enjoyed learning the catechism. I now know it came from a book called the Westminster Shorter Catechism which dates back to a time soon after the Reformation in England. It consists of a series of questions and answers summarising the main principles of the Christian faith. The vicar would read out each question and if it was a new one for us he would try to explain it. He wrote the answer on the blackboard after which we would repeat in unison and endeavour to memorise it. By working at this regularly, we all got a thorough academic knowledge of Bible doctrine.

The first catechism we learned has always stayed with me and been both a challenge and an inspiration over the years:

The question goes like this: *What is the chief purpose of man?* Or as it was explained to us: Why are we here on this earth?

The answer: *To glorify God and enjoy him for ever.*

As I think back to my school days, I realise my formal education was very limited. We did learn to read, write and do simple arithmetic, we also had a nature table and were encouraged to bring to school any plants, flowers, bird's eggs, caterpillars or other natural things that caught our interest in the hedgerows. However, more importantly, the basic biblical explanations offered us for our very existence, (if we would but take it to heart), laid the perfect foundation for the life God intended us to live both here in time and in eternity. I must say that as a child it didn't mean much to me, but since then, I've often brought to mind what I was taught. It has raised all sorts of questions for me over the years, particularly in regard to what it means to glorify God, but it also encouraged me to believe that God wants me to enjoy a relationship with Him and not be frightened by seeing him merely as a taskmaster.

An amusing incident in one of those lessons with the vicar comes readily to mind. The Rev. Devenar would often pounce on individuals with a random catechism question and expect the correct response. One lad, Albert, was never too quick off the mark and being confronted with the question: *In what condition did God create Adam and Eve?* He faltered and then blurted out, 'Was it raining?'

The Rev. Devenar wasn't amused and made him stand in the corner of the classroom for the rest of the lesson. Of course the correct answer was: *God made Adam and Eve perfect and without sin.*

Girl's long dress

As a little girl I often envied my brothers. Richard was less than three years older than me and then there was John just seventeen months my senior. Samuel my next brother had then come along about eighteen months after me. I was therefore surrounded by boys all dressed in breeches and it galled me considerably to have to wear a long dress down to my ankles. Breeches enabled boys to run around, climb trees, sit astride ponies and do all the things I would love to have done without the encumbrance of such a long dress.

I remember asking Mum why I couldn't wear breeches.

'Because you are a girl,' she had answered, smiling at me. 'Girls are special. God made us to support the men and to produce babies for them.'

'But why should that affect what we wear? I answered, frowning.

Mum thought for a bit before answering. 'I suppose our clothes reflect our different roles in life,' she said. 'Boys and men do the active things outside the house so they need clothes that enable them to move about freely. We girls and women keep the home fires burning, nurse the men when they get injured and I must say, sometimes have to sort out the mess they make of relationships.

I had to be content with this but I did wonder why we couldn't wear breeches under our dresses. That would help a lot. I must have been a bit ahead of my time in thinking like this because these days, women wear bloomers which are not too unlike under-breeches. When I was growing up, girls wore nothing between their legs. Under our long dresses, we sometimes wore a wrap-around garment called a shift but that was all. Clothing to pull over our legs was beginning to come into fashion – they were called 'drawers'. I later wore a pair of these, there was a separate one for each leg, held up by a support around the waist; they failed however, to cover between the legs.

Chapter 4

Childhood Adventures

O ccasionally nowadays, I hear children saying they are bored. As farming children, when we were young, I can categorically say, we were never bored. Firstly, we each had our daily jobs to do, either in the house or on the farm, and secondly, there was so much of interest in the world around us.

I was greatly influenced by my brothers in how I occupied my time. We loved to explore the countryside and would roam the fields searching for new and interesting animals, plants and insects. The diversity of God's amazing creation never failed to thrill me, although I must say as children, we took it far too much for granted. We collected butterflies, moths and birds' eggs; Dad and Mum were always willing to help us identify them. In time, we ourselves became quite the authority on various species of flora and fauna native to the Sussex meadows and woodland. I loved to watch the birds and was content to sit for hours in some chosen spot waiting for them to emerge from their hidey holes in the hedgerows, trees and growing crops. The boys didn't usually have the same patience, but often by watching quietly, I could give them a better idea of where to find the particular bird's nests they were looking for. We always tried our best not to disturb the nests more than necessary and would only take one egg from a hatch. This didn't seem to worry the birds unduly and the parent bird would usually soon return to continue keeping her progeny warm and snug as they developed inside their pretty eggshells.

I remember one evening Dad suddenly announced that he thought we had lapwings nesting in the upper field.

'Have you seen the nest Dad?' asked Richard excitedly.

'No, but I saw a lapwing doing acrobats in the air this morning, which I believe is the way a male tries to impress his female mate. We often have lapwings feeding on the land in winter but they have usually moved on somewhere else by now, so it looks as though this pair is staying.'

'Wow, I'd love to have a lapwing's egg in my collection,' exclaimed Richard.' Do you know what they look like?'

Dad explained that he had come across a nest some years earlier and the eggs were more pointed than those of most birds and rather attractively speckled.

'What struck me,' he continued, 'was the way all four eggs were arranged in the nest. The narrower,

Lapwing

fairly pointed ends all faced neatly into the centre forming a tight circle.'

'I guess that enabled mother lapwing to cover them better and ensure they kept warm,' Mum added.

The next day I finished my chores before the boys and set off across the farm to try and find the lapwings and hopefully their nest. It was lovely to sense that spring was now well and truly with us. There was a softness in the air and plenty of signs of growth were all around me. I skirted around the hops field, new shoots were already beginning to seek out the poles to clamber upwards on and made my way across to the upper field where wheat, sown the previous autumn, was now sprouting. I'd heard people say that Dad was a good farmer and certainly the fields and hedgerows all looked well cared for.

'*Now,*' I said to myself, '*where are those lapwings?*'

I settled myself down on a tree stump in the corner of the field and waited. Within about ten minutes, a black and white bird about the size of a crow but quite different in shape, took off from the middle of the field. It had rather wide, rounded wings and began soaring around above the field, diving suddenly and then swooping upwards again. As it swooped, its shrill call filled the air, a two-toned call, the first part more drawn out and then finishing fairly abruptly on a higher note – peeer wit, peeer wit. I suddenly remembered that another name for this bird was based on this call, 'peewit'.

I was fairly inconspicuous in the corner of the field in my dark clothes and as long as I kept motionless, I didn't think the bird would be able to see me. After a while, it came back to rest in the field and I had a good view of it. The most outstanding feature was a surprisingly long narrow crest sticking up from its head. I'd seen lapwings at a distance before but never as close as this. It wandered away from me through the low growing wheat and when it stopped, I realised that it was standing near a second bird that was squatting amongst the green undergrowth. I concluded that the site of the nest must be hidden right there. I decided it best not to disturb the two birds and after a while crept away as quietly as possible.

As I walked back home I debated whether or not I would tell Richard and John what I'd found. The lapwings were such lovely birds and I felt it a privilege to have them nesting in our field. '*Let Richard and John find the nest themselves if they can,*' I said to myself. '*I'll not help them this time.*'

Later that day the boys reported on their own efforts to find the lapwings' nest, for the purpose of adding another egg to their collection. Their experience was rather amusing.

'Those birds are amazing,' Richard began. 'As we approached the field, one of them swooped down at us out of the sky.'

'It was really dangerous,' added John. 'It kept swooping within an inch or two of our heads screaming loudly.'

'We tried to ignore it,' continued Richard, 'but this was virtually impossible as it kept coming back again and again.'

'Then we saw the other bird on the ground,' said John, interrupting his brother. 'But it was acting so strangely.'

'Yes,' said Richard. 'One wing was all floppy as if it was broken. The bird kept looking back at us over its shoulder as it moved away slowly through the wheat. We searched for the nest as best as we could, but knowing Dad would be angry if we trod down too much wheat, we couldn't look very thoroughly.'

'And all the time the first bird was screaming at us and aiming for our heads,' continued John. 'In the end we were pleased to escape without injury.'

Dad laughed and laughed and laughed.

Apparently this was all typical behaviour for lapwings and Dad thinks that its name is due to the female's habit of trailing one of her wings in an attempt to draw predators away from her nest. She's making herself appear easy prey herself by pretending to be injured. Once she had drawn a fox or stoat or whatever far enough away from the nest, she would then fly off out of harm's way. Our Creator God has given his creatures all sorts of wonderful, instinctive behaviour traits and as I've got older I've learned to marvel at his wisdom and creative skill. As the Bible declares, *the whole earth is full of his glory* [2]

I don't think the boys were ever able to add a lapwing's egg to their collection.

---

[2] Isaiah 6:3

Chapter 5

More Childhood Adventures

Mum was always most appreciative when we were able to bring her home a rabbit or two. Since Dad had shown the boys how to set snares, I remember the thrill of hunting and setting our wits against those of the poor rabbit giving me as much excitement as it did Richard and John.

The local ironmongers sold rabbit wire, which is a fine twined wire of several strands, making it perfectly flexible and exceedingly strong. To catch our rabbit, we needed to make a suitably sized noose with the wire, large enough for the rabbit to get its head into but not the whole body. The noose was then set up two or three

Rabbit snare

inches above the ground in a well-worn rabbit run at the edge of a field where the longish grass abounded. It could be supported in position by a sturdy twig or plant stem. The other end of the wire was then attached to a wooden peg which needed to be firmly hammered into the ground.

Rabbits tend to use the same well-worn tracks in and out of fields and it's fairly easy to identify such 'runs'.

We would set two or three snares in different runs late in the day and then come out as soon as we could in the morning to see whether any poor, unfortunate rabbit had been caught. Often the animal would be dead in the snare having been strangled by the noose around its neck. But sometimes it would still be alive and this I dreaded. Thankfully Dad had shown the boys how to quickly and humanely kill rabbits and fowl. I won't go into any details.

Richard and John would always ensure they had sharp pocket knives with them when we were hunting rabbits. Dad had taught all of us how to gut and clean both rabbits and chickens, as he considered this a necessary skill for country life. It is easier to do this rather gruesome task with rabbits when the animal is still warm and we would always try to take rabbits back home to Mum which had already been gutted. The whole family thoroughly enjoyed rabbit pie.

The boys also liked to keep the rabbit skins. After successful removal from the animal and scraped clean, the skins were soaked in salt water for a few days then pulled out and nailed to a board to dry. The dried skins, having been cured by the salt, could then be cut to shape and sewn together to make mats for our bedrooms. Occasionally after the hunt had caught a fox on our land, we were able to get a larger animal to skin and red fox skins made a rather more attractive carpet than the grey rabbit ones. The trouble was, if the dogs weren't immediately called off when they caught a fox, there sadly wasn't much of the animal left to skin.

Snaring rabbits and hunting foxes might sound cruel to those not living in the country, but on the farm, rabbits were a pest, demolishing the grass in the hay fields and the young cereal shoots; foxes loved to prey on our hens if given half a chance.

We were constantly plagued by mice and rats in the farmyard and barns so we employed several farm cats which, to a greater or less degree kept the pests at bay, but occasionally Dad needed to call in the services of the rat man to deal with the vermin. With his ferrets and a little fox terrier, they managed to oust a fair number of rats from their nesting places; the little dog was extremely quick and efficient at catching them. The rat man was paid on the basis of the number of dead bodies he could show Dad. Dad always checked the bodies to ensure they hadn't been dead very long and insisted the dead rats stayed with us to dispose of, as he suspected the rat man had a little supply he took around with him to boost his wages.

One year when the rat number had increased out of all proportion, the boys had the idea they could catch some themselves. Richard had heard of a method using snares similar to those we used for rabbits but with one essential variation, the caught rat was left hanging up in the tree. When he told us this, it sounded so intriguing that I made sure I was in on the act.

The wire needed to be thinner and finer than that for a rabbit snare and of course the noose smaller, but instead of anchoring the noose to the ground it was connected via a wooden peg and a piece of string to a pliant branch of a nearby tree. The peg needed to have a substantial triangle notch cut out of it and then a second peg prepared with a similar-sized notch but in the opposite direction. The second peg was then fastened firmly into the ground in a suitable position near a rat run and immediately under the bendy tree branch. Of course the problem was to find a rat run under a suitable tree. Next, having fastened the peg with the wire noose attached to it to the branch, we pulled down the branch and anchored it in the bent position by means of the two pegs, the triangular notch on the one pulling against the triangular notch on the other. If arranged correctly, the noose to catch the rat should be positioned accurately at ground level in the rat run. The aim was when a rat ran into the noose it would cause the peg to which the wire noose was attached, to move away from its position and the branch would then spring up taking the rat in the noose along with it.

The boys had great fun putting the whole thing together, but how to make the rat run into the noose was the question. Rats seemed far more intelligent than rabbits and don't willingly put their necks into nooses.

The whole thing required further thought. Actually I think it was me who made the suggestion which proved to be the solution.

'We need to frighten the rat whilst it's running in the direction of the noose,' I said. 'If it's running in fright it won't perhaps notice the noose.'

The boys persuaded Dad to let them have a ferret. It was, after all, for a good cause; controlling the rat population without the expense of paying the rat man.

Having a ferret gave hunting a new impetus. We could also use Billy, (the name we gave our ferret), for catching rabbits as well as rats.

Billy the ferret

The boys set up a snare in a rat run coming out of a pile of brush wood. We then introduced Billy the ferret into the wood pile on the opposite side and lo and behold, before we could say 'Jack Robinson', a rat was hanging by its neck from the tree. The boys then had to secure it in an old sack, having added a heavy stone and drown it in the water butt.

Our hunting pursuits led us into many more adventures and I might have one or two more stories later.

Chapter 6

Loving God?

Richard and John were mostly good friends to me and little Samuel would often tag along with us when we roamed around the fields. Not that we had a lot of time for this, as school and our home chores took up most of each day. However, I well remember a time, when I was about seven, when the boys had been very nasty to me about something. I can't actually remember now what it was, but the resentment had so festered in my mind that I had convinced myself that I hated them.

One morning when all this was happening, Dad read a passage from the Bible at breakfast prayers which said: *'He that loveth not his brother whom he hath seen, how can he love God whom he hath not seen?*[3]*'*

Oh dear, this really spoke to my conscience. As I lay awake in bed that night I reasoned with myself about how to try and excuse my attitude. *'God is kind,'* I thought. *'My brothers have been horrible to me so surely hating them doesn't mean I'm not loving God?'*

Then there came the burning question: *'Do I love God?'* The more I thought about this the more confused I got. I just didn't know whether I did or not. I loved my mother. Even when she was angry

---

[3] 1 John 4:20

with me I knew she loved me and I knew without any doubt, that I loved her. But loving God? How could I love God? I didn't know him. Yes, I knew things about him but they were all second hand: things that Dad and Mum had told me from the Bible. I didn't know God himself.

'Dare I ask Mum about this?' I thought. *'Would she laugh at me?'* Somehow it seemed so important to me but I couldn't bear the thought of being misunderstood and laughed at.

It was some days before I plucked up enough courage to talk to Mum about my fears. I had been helping her in the kitchen and she had given me the task of making rock cakes. Mum mostly liked to use our own produce in her cooking but occasionally we were able to buy imported dried fruit from the grocer and then simple rock cakes made with flour, baking powder, butter, eggs, sugar and dried fruit became a family favourite. The girls were making butter in the dairy so I had Mum to myself.

'Mum,' I said rather shyly, 'how can I love God?'

My mother looked at me a little startled but after a moment or two said, 'Ruth, dear, we need the Holy Spirit to enable us to love God.' Then perhaps realising that this answer wasn't going to help me much added, 'I'll tell you what has helped me to love him.'

She then went on to tell me that by thinking about God in everyday things, and recognising that all we have comes from him for our enjoyment, had helped her to worship him and love him.

'For instance,' she continued, 'when I go out to feed the chickens, I make a conscious effort to thank him for another new day; I breathe in the fresh air and praise him for giving me health and strength, my husband and children. I thank him for the farm and the animals.

'For me,' said Mum, 'acknowledging God and talking to him has been a good way to start learning to love him. But later I realised that there is a far greater reason to love him. God sent his Son Jesus to die for us and to be our Saviour. He has so loved us that he has taken all the bad behaviour of his children on himself and borne the punishment for it. The Apostle John wrote: *We love him, because he first loved us.* [4] Think about that my dear and ask God to show himself to you and as you begin to know him you will certainly love him.'

I took these thoughts away with me and tried to remember to think about God more and to thank him for each new day as Mum had said.

Soon after this, we learned a new song at school. Miss Read said it was written by an Irish lady who was the wife of an Anglican clergyman. It went like this:

All things bright and beautiful,
All creatures great and small,
All things wise and wonderful
The Lord God made them all.

I learned several verses of this hymn and by singing them to myself as often as I could, mostly when out in the open air, going down the lane to school or doing things on the farm, it helped me sense God's presence and I believe it certainly helped me to begin loving Him.

---

[4] 1 John 4:19

Chapter 7

More Brothers and Sisters

As I look back now, a mother myself and also having read Mum's writings, I'm quite amazed at the inner strength, patience and perseverance that Selina, my mother, demonstrated throughout her life. Sadly, she was recognised by most people who knew us, merely as the wife of Eli Page without any real identity of her own. When in the presence of her husband, whether that was at home with the family or in the company of others, she said precious little. However when she did speak, she showed a depth of wisdom that few others seemed to possess.

I have realised in recent years that people, many in fact, seem to go through life blinkered. We sometimes put blinkers on horses when they are pulling a cart or trap to stop them seeing anything except what is straight in front of them. Some horses are easily frightened or distracted and need protecting in this way. However, many human beings appear to have self-imposed blinkers. They see only those things that concern themselves and have very little sensitivity towards others, little ability to empathise or see things from another point of view. My mother was not blinkered. She loved people and seemed able to place herself in other people's shoes. This gave her the ability to speak in a helpful way and when asked, to give salient advice. We children learned to value this and would far more readily go to mother than father with our questions and worries.

Whilst at Limden farm, our family expanded rapidly. Mum bore child after child, which to us at that time in a farming environment, seemed the natural thing to happen.

Samuel, Mum and Dad's third son, was born on 18th December 1842, seventeen and a half months after my birthday on 2nd July 1841. Then Orpah arrived on 10th September 1844 with Naomi following on 16th July 1846. For many parents six healthy children would be considered quite an adequate family but when number seven arrived on 13th May 1848 Dad and Mum named him Ebenezer, the biblical Hebrew word meaning 'hitherto has the Lord helped us'. Whether intentional or not, the name implies there were still more to come and so it was. Mercy arrived on 18th February 1850 and Mary on 1st December 1851 and then prior to our move from Limden Farm to Perching Manor, Mum had also given us Elizabeth, born on 7th October 1853 and Dorcas on 17th February 1856.

Being the oldest daughter, Mum gave me quite a lot of responsibility in caring for my younger siblings. One thing I remember that amazed me as a child was the fact that as sister after sister arrived in the family home, they were all quite unique. Each was a personality in her own right and needed individual understanding and care as a result. Dad was always very busy outside on the farm, and later away preaching as well, so Mum gave me clear instruction that the men worked outside and we women and girls looked after the house and the babies. I did point out to her that it wasn't altogether fair because we had some outside work to do too. For instance, the girls generally dealt with the hens, also the milk and cream in the dairy was our responsibility. Making butter was hard work but this was mostly a job for our two house girls, Eliza and Sarah, and when they moved on, we employed a dairy girl who came in each day from Stonegate. Mum, however, always had to oversee this dairy work and was prepared to take it over if she felt it would be better for the girls to be doing something else. It was Mum and not the girls who taught me how to make butter and even as young as five, I often took a turn at churning the milk.

I had just had my fifth birthday when Naomi arrived and she was the first sibling that I actually was aware of the preparation for and lead up to her birth. In my childish understanding, Samuel and Orpah had just suddenly arrived overnight. A stork might have brought them as far as I knew. But Mum shared with me the fact that Naomi was going to be born and I remember the excitement of realising that a new baby was developing inside her. I think this birth must have been one of the most difficult for Mum. Grandma came to look after us and Mum stayed upstairs in bed for several days. I recollect Dad saying at some point later, that Mara might have been a more appropriate name for Naomi, his implication being that her birth had been a particular bitter one for Mum.[5]

Mum's response was so typical of her: 'Eli,' she said, 'you are forgetting the Scripture that says a mother soon forgets the pain of childbirth for the joy that a new child is born into the world. My *bitterness* is past and we have a lovely baby girl. We can call her Naomi with pride, for God has truly given us a *pleasant* child.'

Mum always fed her babies herself until they were at least six months old and sometimes older, then she would slowly begin to supplement her own milk with some solids like porridge. At this stage she would look to me to help feed my baby siblings.

After the births of Orpah and Naomi, a baby brother arrived and I was nearly seven when little Ebenezer was born. I think this was just the right age to appreciate another baby and Ebenezer became very special to me. I was allowed to rock him to sleep and Mum also showed me how to bath him. I learned how to test the temperature of the water with my elbow and although at first Mum always wanted to check it herself, she soon trusted me to get it right myself. You can imagine what a terrible shock it was to me when little Eb died. He had his first birthday on 13th May and then at the end of June about a month later God took him from us. I've already told you a bit of how Eb's death affected me but there's something else too, something far more positive.

---

[5] In Hebrew Mara means bitter but Naomi means pleasant. See the biblical reference to this in Ruth 1:20

Chapter 8

Is this God Speaking?

As a little girl, my favourite Bible story was that of my namesake Ruth in the Old Testament. Mum would regularly tell us stories from the Bible and I simply loved those winter evenings when we would sit cosily at Mum's feet around the kitchen fire. We knew Mum loved these Bible stories and her faith in God combined with a real enthusiasm for his word, was a powerful influence on us all as children. When at last it was time for bed, she would conclude with a brief prayer and we would have to brave the chill of the cold house and hurry upstairs to our beds, the older ones carrying candles to light the way.

Sometimes Mum would ask us for a choice of story so whenever it was my turn, I would usually ask to hear again about Ruth from the country of Moab. Soon after the death of my brother Eb, the story took on a new meaning for me as I began to feel I could really identify with my namesake and in a remarkable way this comforted me.

Ruth of long ago had lost her husband when she was still a young lady and now I had lost the boy I loved, my little brother. What encouraged me in my childish understanding was the fact that God had eventually given Ruth another husband, a rich farmer named Boaz and also a little baby son. This gave me hope that if I trusted God like

Ruth had done, one day he would give me someone else to love and perhaps a baby of my own who I could call Ebenezer.

I thought about this often and then one day God showed me something even more wonderful.

In our family prayers Dad was reading the first chapter of Matthew's Gospel which lists the family tree of Jesus. I wasn't listening very carefully, but suddenly, I heard the name Ruth. Dad didn't like us interrupting but I just had to ask him about this, so when he had finished reading and praying I burst out, 'Dad, did you read the name Ruth? Is this my special Ruth, the lady from Moab?'

Dad found the verse again and read it to me: *And Salmon begat Boaz of Rachab; and Boaz begat Obed of Ruth; and Obed begat Jesse; and Jesse begat David the king.*[6]

'Yes, my dear,' he said, your Ruth, as you like to call her, was the great grandmother of King David and many years later, Jesus, known as the Son of David, was also a descendent of Ruth.'

'*Wow*,' I thought to myself, '*I wonder if that is a message for me*'.

That night in bed I thought over these amazing facts and talked to God about them.

'Lord Jesus,' I prayed, 'I believe you've shown me that you are going to give me a husband and children like you did for Ruth of old. I do pray that my children and their families will know your special blessing and like Ruth's family, will be part of your purpose to extend your kingdom and bring blessing to this world.'

---

[6] Matthew 1:5

Chapter 9

Bee Keeping

The countryside around us was bursting with life and I loved it. For Mum, spring was a special time and her enthusiasm was infectious. Going out for a walk with Mum was always an adventure as there were many exciting discoveries to be made: the first primrose in the hedgerow; the beautiful brimstone butterfly enticed out of hibernation by the April sunshine; the early arrival home of our farmyard swallows after their winter sojourn in Africa; the first call of the cuckoo. It must have been an effort for Mum to get out of the house and leave the constant house work, but somehow most weeks she managed it. She had a little trolley that she would pull the babies along in and she taught us, when we came to the perfect spot, how to sit quietly on a fallen tree or a grassy bank and just watch. For Mum this was God's world, created firstly for his own glory and secondly for our benefit and it was she who trained us to use our eyes to appreciate it.

One sunny day in May, I remember being introduced to the world of the amazing honey bee. We were sitting on a fallen tree, Mum was surrounded by five, small, alert children and the ten month old Naomi asleep in the little cart. There was the pink flowering vetch and clover in the grass around us and we could hear a constant hum as bees flitted from one blossom to another.

'Watch and listen to the bees,' said Mum, 'they are happily doing their shopping.'

Bee on clover

Sensing there was a new story to come, Richard whispered, 'tell us about them Mum.'

'They are collecting pollen and nectar from the flowers to take home to feed their babies and make honey for the winter,' explained Mum. 'God has given the bees little shopping bags on their back legs. Don't try and touch them because they can sting you if they get angry, but just look very carefully, you'll see as they fly from flower to flower that their back legs are getting fatter and fatter as they push pollen down into the little bags.'

'Does each bee have its own little home somewhere?' asked Richard excitedly.

'Oh no,' answered Mum. 'Bees live in communities. The boss bee is bigger than the others and is known as the queen.'

'That must mean the boss is female,' I said. 'That's interesting. Is there a king bee too?'

'Actually no,' answered Mum smiling. 'Bee families are quite different from ours. There are male bees which are called drones, but they have just one purpose in life and are certainly not the bosses. In fact, when winter comes the females will drive them away to die in the cold because otherwise they would eat up all the honey.'

'But that wouldn't be fair if they had helped collect the honey,' said John with a worried look on his face.

'But that's just what they don't do,' responded Mum. 'They are lazy and don't really do any work at all. Look at all these busy bees flying around from flower to flower collecting nectar. They are all females and are known as the worker bees. The males don't help them at all.'

'But that's terrible,' I said. 'Our daddy works hard and even if he didn't we wouldn't turn him out into the cold in winter.'

'You said the male bees just have one purpose,' said Richard, 'is that just to be daddies to the baby bees, like we get Eric the big bull to mate with the cows? Daddy explained that to me,' he added with a slightly embarrassed look.

Mum was silent for a bit and seemed to be wondering what to say until John broke the silence. 'Does each of these bees have a husband and their own babies back in their home?' he asked.

'No, as I said,' smiled Mum, 'bees are very different from us, they live together in a community, the queen bee is the boss and she lays all the eggs. The female worker bees are like the house maids and do all the work. They make delicate wax cradles for the queen to lay the eggs in and then they look after the little grubs that hatch out of the eggs, feeding them until they become adult bees. Other worker bees collect all the food from the flowers and what is not needed to feed the babies, is stored in little wax containers which we call honeycomb. When I was a child, we kept bees for a while and my father, your grandfather, explained all this to me.'

'I would like to keep bees,' said Richard thoughtfully.

It was some years before Richard got his wish fulfilled. One evening when he was about twelve, Dad showed him how to make a bee skep out of straw. Richard then made four skeps of his own and almost immediately, we were able to get bee swarms, (a queen bee with her many worker bee courtiers), to make their home in two of them.

What seemed rather unpleasant was the fact that in order to get the honey in the autumn, we had to gas the bees and break up the straw skep. This was until Dad heard of a much more sensible innovation.

Bee skep

Instead of having a single straw skep, each skep was made up of two compartments. Above the larger compartment, where the queen lived and laid her eggs, was a second smaller compartment separated from the lower one by a piece of wood with holes bored in it. The holes were big enough for the worker bees to crawl through but too small for the more sizable queen to wriggle through. Because the worker bees seemed happy to use the upper compartment as a larder to store their honey in, we were able to take this away at the end of the season and leave the main skep intact. This avoided the need to kill all the bees and we simply gave them a sugary substance as a food substitute to keep them alive over the winter.

Chapter 10

Battles

One evening after supper and prayers, Dad produced something unusual from his pocket resembling a small stone and asked us what we thought it was. Richard stretched out his hand for it and Dad passed it over to him.

Richard examined it carefully and then gave his verdict. 'It's a piece of flint, Dad,' he said.

We were all familiar with flint as it occurs frequently in larger or smaller pieces on our chalk hills. It was often used to add some decorative relief to the red brick walls of some of the village houses.

Arrowhead

'True,' answered Dad, 'but this is no random piece of flint, it's had some use in the distant past.'

'Was it some form of tool?' responded John, taking it from Richard. 'It's certainly got a sharp point but it's very small for a tool, perhaps it was part of something else.'

Mum looked across the table smiling. 'I remember your grandfather showing us a piece of flint like that when we were children,' she said. 'He found it amongst the carrots he was pulling up in the garden.'

'I think I might guess what it is,' I said rather shyly. 'Is it an arrowhead? Miss Read told us that in the past the archers would use sharp pieces of flint to head their arrows for hunting and fighting.'

'Good girl,' said Dad. 'It's great to know that village school taught you some local history.'

Richard and John took a renewed interest in the small object. 'Where did you find it, Dad?' Richard asked. 'Maybe we could find some more and make some arrows ourselves.'

'These things come to the surface very occasionally when we plough the fields,' Dad replied. 'You can keep your eyes open for them but it's fairly rare to actually find them. My eye caught this one as we were sowing wheat this afternoon.'

'I'd like to take it to show Miss Read,' I said. 'She might be able to tell us more about it.'

Dad was happy for me to take the little piece of flint to show my former school teacher, for although I had by then left school, I was sure Miss Mary Read would be glad to see me and share more of her knowledge about such things.

One of our neighbouring farmers was William Read. He was unmarried and lived with three of his sisters in Stonegate Farm House. Two sisters ran the home but Mary Read was the teacher at Stonegate's National School. She was somewhat older than my own parents but very approachable, and since leaving school I had always found her most friendly. I would sometimes meet my younger siblings from school and Miss Read always had a kind word for me, I knew she took an interest in all her former pupils.

Miss Read was indeed very interested in and thrilled about the arrowhead. 'It's a lovely example of ancient workmanship Ruth,' she said, her eyes sparkling. 'Flint can be split to make a very sharp point and notice the short, narrow shaft on the non-pointed end, this would have been slotted onto the wooden arrow. The hunters and archers would have used glue made from tree resin to hold it in place.'

'I would love to borrow it for a few days to show the children' she added. 'Do you think your father would mind, Ruth?'

'I'm sure he would be more than happy,' I answered. 'I'll come and pick it up again next week.'

I thought a lot about that arrowhead in the next few days and tried to imagine the men who had made it and used it for hunting. When I returned to Stonegate School to collect it, I had a lot of questions for Miss Read.

'The village of Fletching, just north of Uckfield, near Sheffield Park, was a major producer of bows and arrows in medieval times,' said Miss Read. 'In fact that's how the village got its name as the French word for arrow is *flèche*. It's quite likely this arrowhead was shaped by the skilled workmen right there in Fletching.'

'Do you think this arrowhead was used in hunting or in battle?' I asked.

'Because of the location where it was found, most probably hunting,' answered Miss Read. There would have been wild boar in the forests around here so such an arrowhead would have been strong enough for shooting them with.

'However, we shouldn't forget that there have been some significant battles in East Sussex,' Miss Read added. 'The town of Battle was so called because of its proximity to the site of the so-called Battle of Hastings when our English King Harold was defeated by William of Normandy on 14th October 1066. The pope at the time, instructed William to build an abbey as penance for the many lives lost that day - Battle Abbey, around which the town of Battle was established.

'A lesser known local battle here in Sussex was the Battle of Lewes,' Miss Read continued. 'King Henry III had provoked the English Barons by his autocratic behaviour, even after his father, King John, had been forced to sign the Magna Carta in 1215. Simon de Montfort, Earl of Leicester, represented the barons and an army under his leadership defeated King Henry and his son Edward in the Battle of Lewes, 14th May 1264. The King and Prince Edward were imprisoned and for eighteen months before his death, at the Battle of Evesham,

Simon de Montfort governed England in their name. The Sussex town of Fletching had been Simon de Montfort's headquarters before the battle, and the bows and arrows seen in the Lewes Town Council's oil painting of the battle were almost certainly made in that very town.' [7]

'Fancy an army fighting their own king,' I commented. 'Can that be right?'

'The people of Flimwell would have most certainly supported the barons,' answered Mary Read.

'When you say the people of Flimwell, do you mean our Flimwell? Near Ticehurst? I questioned, gasping in astonishment. 'What did they have against King Henry III?'

'Well,' answered Miss Read, 'Henry felt threatened. He was on his way to confront Simon de Montfort at Lewes and had stopped at Flimwell. There he learned that his cook had been killed. He suspected that one or more of the Flimwell villagers were guilty and were on the side of his enemy, the barons. He had no time for an investigation, so simply instructed his army to take 300 villagers into a neighbouring field and cut off their heads. The field and surrounding area is now known as Yellowcoat Wood and if you think about it, 300 people would have been the population of most of Flimwell and perhaps of the outlying farms as well.' [8]

As I walked home clutching my arrowhead, I couldn't help wondering what stories this small piece of flint could tell me if only it could talk.

---

[7] https://en.wikipedia.org/wiki/Battle_of_Lewes
[8] http://orig.villagenet.co.uk/?v=flimwell_east%20sussex

Chapter 11

May Bugs

Another incident which comes to mind as I think back over my childhood at Limden Farm, was the year we had a greater invasion than normal of May bugs or Billy witches as we sometimes called them. Most years during late spring and early summer, we had these large beetles flying around at dusk. Some years they were more prolific than others and that one year in particular, I remember it felt as though we were experiencing one of the plagues of Egypt.

May bug

Dad was always upset to see Billy witches and we were instructed to catch and kill as many as we could.

'Why Dad?' I asked, 'do they hurt us?

'No Ruth,' Dad answered, 'they are quite harmless to us but they lay a lot of eggs in the ground and when the grubs develop they eat roots and crops like potatoes causing a lot of damage.'

Mary Read told us more about these impressive insects and as with most aspects of God's wonderful creation, such facts fascinated me. Their real name is the Common Cockchafer. They are not very pleasant when they are flying around you but Miss Read asked us to try and catch a few in a jam jar and bring them to school alive so we could examine them and she could tell us more about them. I managed to get a decent, live specimen as did several other children, so the next day at school we had about twelve living beetles to study.

As you no doubt already know, May bugs are about an inch long, brownish and when not flying, their delicate wings are tucked away under protective outer wing cases. Our teacher wanted us to examine them more closely.

'Look carefully at their heads,' directed Miss Read. 'Can you see their antennae or feelers? You know what a butterfly's feeler looks like with a little knob at the end, what is different about the May bug's antennae?'

'My beetle looks as though it has a little hand with fingers at the end of each feeler,' commented my friend Sophia after we all had adequate time to examine our specimens.

'Yes ours too,' the responses rippled around the classroom.

'Good,' said Miss Read. 'We often call those little finger-like protrusions 'leaves' rather than fingers but good that's exactly what I wanted you to see. Now I want you to count the number of leaves or fingers at the end of each antenna.'

This wasn't so easy to do as the insects kept scuttling around, but it was generally agreed that the beetles had at least six 'leaves' and some children said theirs had seven. I counted the 'leaves' at the end of each antenna of my beetle several times, and was convinced it had seven. I was adamant that those who said six weren't counting properly and were wrong. However Miss Read then said something which helped to teach me a lesson which I've tried to apply to other situations as I've gone through life, namely never jump to conclusions about other people without being doubly sure of all the facts.

'The male beetles have seven 'leaves,' she told us, 'and the females only six.'

'So that's it,' I said to myself, 'That means mine is a male. I'll call him Billy.'

Miss Read then went on to explain much more about the insect which was plaguing our countryside in such huge numbers that year.

She told us that the fully developed adult beetles live for only about six weeks, during which time they will mate and the female lays up to eighty eggs in several batches under the surface of the soil. After three to four weeks, the eggs hatch into white grubs which burrow into the soil and live there for three or four years. During this time, they munch away on roots and tubers, growing to about an inch and a half. Then early in the autumn they will pupate. That means turning into a pupa, like a butterfly caterpillar turns into a chrysalis. The adult beetle will then emerge from the pupa before winter but will remain underground until the warm weather in the spring draws it to the surface.

There were all sorts of stories about the May bugs that year. Some gypsy boys came by the farm with a number of beetles flying around their heads. 'They had them attached to lengths of cotton,' said Richard, who had watched them pass by. 'I think they must somehow tie the cotton around one of the beetle's legs. I suppose it's like flying a living kite. They were selling them for four a penny but I said I would make my own if I really wanted one.'

Mum then told us that when she was young, someone in the village of Ripe, where she lived, had a recipe for preparing a meal of May beetles.

'Ugh!' I commented. 'I wouldn't want to eat them.'

'But John the Baptist ate locusts,' said John. 'I wonder what beetles would taste like. Do you know how the lady cooked them, Mum?'

'I seem to remember your grandmother telling me that you should cut away the legs and wings, fry them in butter and then add them to a soup. I don't think we'll try it, although the farm workers are catching and killing hundreds of them.'

The flying beetles soon all disappeared, but one evening as I was lying in bed thinking about them, I began to imagine hundreds of little white grubs burrowing in our fields ready to feast on any root crops Dad would sow. *'Then, in three or four years' time, we'll probably have another plague of them,'* I said to myself. [9]

---

[9] With the use of chemical pesticides, cockchafers were virtually exterminated from England in the twentieth century but with the banning of many of these pesticides the insects are now slowly returning to some areas.

Chapter 12

Railways

One of the most dramatic events of my formative years was the advent of the railways. Dad often used to talk about steam engines. Whilst it was all still purely a subject up for discussion, I remember the amount of scepticism about it all, mainly because of a general fear spread amongst the older Christian generation, that this invention would change the world as they knew it, for the worse. Manual labour accompanied by the use of horses and bullocks was the biblical way of living, therefore, surely these loud, ugly machines must be of the devil.

There was however, no holding back the industrial revolution, so when the steam railway engines and the actual construction of railway lines commenced, the scepticism changed to fascination, and fascination to a practical involvement. For centuries our roads had been atrocious. Although it would be true to say, there had been some improvements, we had to acknowledge that travelling from A to B in a straight line along rails, was sheer bliss in comparison to those bone-shaking rides by coach and horse on rut-infested roads.

My brothers became very excited when we heard that a line was being built from Tunbridge Wells to Hastings, passing us at Limden Farm, just about a mile south of Stonegate. Because of the nature of the countryside north west of us, known as the High Weald, the construction of the line necessitated a number of tunnels. The creation of the latter was no mean feat and I heard that the workmen had not been able to keep fully to the specifications given to them. On 1st September 1851, our most local station Ticehurst Road was opened. Interestingly the station was initially called Witherenden after its nearest hamlet, but this place name meant nothing to most travellers so it was felt that by involving the more significant town of Ticehurst in the name it would give the station more status. [10]

Soon after the opening of the line, Mum took us four older ones for a ride into Tunbridge Wells. What a special treat for us! We very rarely ventured too far from home and to visit a main town like Tunbridge Wells was like a dream come true -and by train too.

Dad drove us to the station in our pony and trap. He arranged to come and meet us from the return train later in the day. We arrived at Witherenden railway station in plenty of time and waited excitedly for the train. We heard it and saw the smoke long before it came spluttering into view. Richard and John ran down the platform to greet the smoking, puffing green monster. They thought it was wonderful. I held mother's hand and Samuel hid behind her, clinging to her skirt, as this huge, mechanical draught-horse came steadily towards us, the whistle blowing.

Once it had stopped it seemed somewhat less frightening. 'Look Mummy,' I cried. 'it has a name. What's it called?'

Mum read out the word inscribed on the side of the monster's shiny round body. 'It's called Ethelbert,' she said.

'What a funny name,' I responded frowning. 'Is she Ethel, a girl engine or Bert a boy engine?'

'I'll tell you about it once we are in the train,' answered Mum. 'Where are the boys?'

Richard and John had run along the entire platform alongside the engine and were now talking to the driver who looked very smart in his pristine uniform.

---

[10] This station was later renamed again as Stonegate

Steam train

'The man says, we can ride with him in the driving place, as far as the next station,' shouted John as he raced back to us.'

'Really?' queried Mum. 'If that's really so, you must be very good boys and keep well out of the way of the fire and the controls.'

Mum, Samuel and I clambered into one of the passenger carriages. There was no one else in the compartment and both Samuel and I were able to sit by the window looking out over the platform. After a few minutes we saw another uniformed man, (who we later heard was called the guard), blow a whistle, wave a red flag and jump into the train at the far end. We were off.

My first ever train journey was exhilarating. Once clear of the station the train seemed to gather considerable speed and the trees and bushes beside the line rushed by. No pony and trap could travel as fast and at first, I began to get quite nervous but Mum assured us it was quite safe so I soon relaxed.

I asked Mum to tell us why the train was named Ethelbert.

'It's an old English name,' Mum said. 'Long ago southern England had a King Ethelbert. Your grandfather, my father, used to tell us about him because he was the first Christian king in England. He was king when the message about Jesus was brought to our island by a missionary from Rome. King Ethelbert was converted to Christianity and ensured that the good news of Jesus dying on the cross for our sins would be spread all over his kingdom of Kent and Wessex.'

'Wow, that was good,' I responded 'I'm so glad our steam engine is called after him. Ethelbert! I quite like that name, maybe I could have a brother called that?'

Mum smiled. 'Probably not,' she said. 'It's a very old fashioned name and today people wouldn't know whether the child was a boy or a girl.'

Suddenly there was a shrill whistle and we realised the train was slowing down. We pulled gently into the next station which Mum told us was Wadhurst. Mum opened the window and waved to the boys who were running along the platform. They scrambled excitedly into the carriage informing us how wonderful a steam engine was and that they both wanted to be train drivers when they grew up.

'There's a very hot fire that makes the steam that makes the engine work,' said Richard, jumping up and down with such enthusiasm. 'There are two drivers and the one keeps putting more coal on the fire while the other man looks after the controls. He told us that the engine uses coal and water. There's a special truck just behind the engine where the coal is kept and some of the stations have a big water tank near the line where, as the man said, the engine can have a drink when it's thirsty.'

'I think steam trains are wonderful,' added John. 'They can go much faster than horses and are much more interesting.'

I couldn't let that statement go unchallenged and retorted with a toss of my head: 'But look at all this horrible smoke. I think horses are much nicer. They are alive. You can talk to horses. They know you. This train journey is great fun but I'd still rather have a horse.'

By now the train was moving off again and Mum very wisely changed the subject by pointing out a hare that was running across the field. We all rushed across to her window to see it and all disagreements about the merits or otherwise of steam trains were forgotten.

Chapter 13

Tunbridge Wells

Having thoroughly enjoyed the visit to Tunbridge Wells, we filled Dad in with all the details, over supper that evening.

'Mum showed us where a famous spring is that has made the town so well-known,' I said. 'She told us that Queen Victoria came to drink from the spring every day, when as a princess she was staying in Tunbridge Wells. But what's so special about that well Dad?' Is it magic?'

Father laughed. 'No, my dear,' he answered. 'It's not magic, but many folk do believe there's something in the Tunbridge Wells water which is good for your health. As you know from our own well, there are reservoirs of water under the ground which originally come from rain and we pump up or collect with buckets. Sometimes when this underground water has soaked slowly through the rocks and soil, it contains minerals absorbed from the rocks. The Tunbridge Wells water has been shown to contain more minerals than most, with a high amount of iron. Our bodies need these minerals so to drink this water can be good for us.'

'If Queen Victoria came all the way from London to drink it,' I responded, 'she must have thought it was very healthy water.'

Dad laughed. 'Tunbridge Wells' water earned a good reputation way back in the very early seventeenth century when a gentleman named Dudley, Lord North, a courtier of King James I, (the king who authorised the translation and use of our English Bible). Anyway this man Dudley, after making himself quite ill through his lifestyle in London, came to recuperate in the Kent countryside and discovered a spring of water. After drinking the water from this spring his health improved so remarkably that he went on to live to the age of eighty. It may or may not have been the water that helped him, but many people then wanted to try the remedy themselves, consequently a town grew up around the spring. Famous people including royalty came to try the water and the town of Tunbridge Wells was established.'

There was silence for a few minutes as we all thought over what Dad had said. Then Richard burst out, 'Mum said that the area around the famous well is called the Pavilion but local people call it the Pantiles. She said there was a story about this which you would tell us.'

Dad looked across at Mum with a smile and took a sip of his beer. 'Yes,' he said 'it's certainly a story worth telling. About a hundred years after the discovery of the spring, although a grand colonnade of shops had been built leading up to the well, called the 'Walk', the ground had obviously not been paved very well. Princess Ann was visiting with her little son the Duke of Gloucester and he unfortunately slipped on the surface around the spring. Princess Ann donated money to pay for better paving but when she next paid a visit, the work had not been done and she was very angry. The town council had to quickly get their heads together and arranged for red clay tiles, which we call pantiles, to be made and laid on the ground to give a good even surface up to and around the spring. As a result, the area was called the Pantiles. Then a few years ago it was considered better to replace the older tiles with larger paving stones and the powers that be, decided the area should now be called the Pavilion. Of course everyone in the town knew it as the Pantiles and continued to call it that. I guess one day, the authorities will give in and revert to its original name.'

'I shall always call it the Pantiles,' I responded with a defiant shake of my head. 'There are a lot of nice little shops there and I wanted to buy a lovely blue silk scarf but Mum said it was too expensive and that I didn't need it.'

Mum indicated that we children could leave the table, but then she turned to Dad and said, 'We saw a newly built chapel by the Pantiles. It was a grand building and was named Rehoboth. Do you know anything about it Eli?'

I, too, had seen the chapel and lingered to hear what Dad had to say.

'Its origin is a very interesting story,' Dad replied. It centres round a Tunbridge Wells tradesman by the name of Thomas Edwards. He's a butcher in Montgomery Place and I've met him occasionally at the markets. Someone introduced me to him as an Independent preacher and we had a drink together. He's about our age. A few years ago he felt God gave him a burden to preach. It seems obvious that he has been anointed with the Holy Spirit in a special way because God has really used him. He started preaching in Mr Carrick's cottage. You remember Mr and Mrs Carrick? They've occasionally come to special services at Burwash. Because the room was small, Mr Henry Carr then offered them a larger room in his house. This also soon became too small to accommodate the growing congregation and they were able to hire the old Mount Sion Chapel, which had been restored and until recently used by the Congregationalists. That church fellowship left once they had opened a new building for themselves in 1848, so Mount Sion Chapel was standing empty and available. The arrangement suited fine until something was said which offended the trustees so they then refused Thomas Edwards any further use of the building. By this time, the group had covenanted together as church members and had formally appointed Thomas Edwards as their pastor. But now they had no building. They used one or two different rooms for a while and eventually erected a marquee to meet in.'

'That would have attracted attention,' exclaimed Mum. It sounds a bit like the tabernacle the children of Israel had in the wilderness at the time of Moses.'

'Yes, but not very convenient,' said Dad. 'But God honoured their commitment and at the end of the very first service in the tent a woman approached Thomas Edwards saying that she knew of a piece of land that would be perfect for a plot on which to build a chapel. She mentioned the land by the Pantiles where they have been now able to build. In telling me this Mr Edwards confessed his lack of faith and said he was very dubious about the possibility of obtaining that particular plot. Anyway, a little later, the owner of the land came into his shop and quite casually, Mr Edwards mentioned their need of a plot of land for a chapel. Amazingly the lady offered them the very piece of land that had been suggested.' [11]

'That's all of God,' said Mum. 'He can move the hearts of anyone in order to fulfil his purpose. What an encouragement that is Eli.'

Rehoboth Chapel

'Yes,' responded Dad smiling, 'and the purchase went through without a hitch and the new chapel named Rehoboth was opened last September.'

---

[11] Ralph Chambers, The Strict Baptist Chapels of England, vol 3, The Chapels of Kent, 1961

'Rehoboth,' said Mum questioningly. 'That name had something to do with a spring of water, didn't it Eli?'

'I'll find the passage,' answered Dad, reaching across for the family Bible that was sitting on the table. 'Yes, here it is in Genesis chapter 26. The story is about Isaac. His father Abraham had dug wells to provide his household and his animals with water but the Philistines had later filled these in. When Isaac dug down nearby and discovered access to the spring, the herdsmen of Gerer claimed the water was theirs. Isaac being a peaceful man moved on and tried digging for water elsewhere. God blessed his work and the new well supplied them with all the water they needed.

'Verse eleven in that chapter reads: *And he removed from thence, and digged another well; and for that they strove not: and he called the name of it Rehoboth; and he said, for now the LORD hath made room for us, and we shall be fruitful in the land.*

'The name Rehoboth actually means a broad place and for Isaac, Rebecca and their household, it was a broad place near a spring of water where they could farm and thrive.'

'An ideal name for Thomas Edward's new church building at the Pantiles in Tunbridge Wells,' said Mum in delight. 'I'd love to go to a special service there one day. Now we've got the new railway line shouldn't that be possible Eli?'

Dad smiled and nodded. 'We'll have to keep our ears to the ground and learn when their pastor's anniversary services are.'

I slipped away after that remembering the words of Jesus that a preacher at our chapel in Burwash had recently used as his text: *'I will build my church and the gates of hell shall not prevail against it.'* [12]

---

[12] Matthew 16:18

Chapter 14

My Friend Sophia

Living on a farm with very few houses around, meant there was very little choice of children to be my friends, apart from my own brothers and younger sisters. However, when I was about eight years old, a new family moved into South Limden Farm. Their name was Harmer. Mum used to occasionally visit Mrs Harmer and when possible I would go with her so I could play with Mrs Harmer's daughter Sophia. I knew Sophia from school because being close in age we were in the same class and sat near each other.

Sophia taught me to appreciate beauty. I guess because the family members around my own age were boys, I tended to be something of a tomboy. Sophia was a real, little girl. She liked dressing as a girl, while I had always felt it unfair that I had to wear a long dress and not breeches like my brothers. I had to sit side saddle on my pony while they could sit astride.

A common love of nature drew us together. We had both learned to identify the most common flowers growing around us in the fields and hedgerows, from our parents and also from Miss Read, at school. However, soon after Sophia and I had become friends, I realised how the delicate colours and different design of the flowers thrilled Sophia even more it seemed than they did me. When I visited her at Lower Limden Farm, she invariably had a new flower to tell me about. She would sometimes pick bunches of blooms of different tones and shades keeping them in water for as long as she could, we both agreed that it was far better to admire them growing in their natural habitat.

I remember one day in particular. We had an excess of raspberries and Mum planned to take some to Ann Harmer, so hoping to see Sophia, I asked to go with her. As soon as she saw us arriving, Sophia ran out to meet us, smiling happily.

'I hoped you would come today,' she shouted. 'I've got something very special to show you.' She dragged me off by the hand and we headed across one of their farm meadows. 'You'll never guess what I've found,' she said. 'It a very special flower but I don't know what it's called, so I want you to ask your Dad. He seems to know everything. My Dad and Mum are just not that interested. One of our farm workers discovered it and showed it to me but he doesn't know its name.'

Sophia remembered exactly where to look and having dragged me to the edge of the field she pointed to a plant growing in the grass. The flower was a light pink and at first I thought there was a brown-looking bee settled on it, then I realised that the bee was actually part of the flower.

'Wow!' I cried 'Isn't that marvellous. Do you think the plant grows the bee to attract real bees?'

'I'd better not pick the flower because there only seems to be one plant here, but I can describe it to my Dad. I wonder if he will know what it's called.' Then I suddenly had an idea. 'We'll show it to my Mum now,' I said to Sophia.

We ran back to the farmhouse and hung around until Mum had finished talking to Sophia's mother, then I persuaded her to come and look at the wonderful plant.

Mum was thrilled when she saw it. 'It's a

Bee orchid

bee orchid,' she said in delight. 'It has been

years since I've seen one. I remember my father showing us one on the South Downs when we were out walking one day. It's really amazing how one part of the flower can grow to look so much like a bee. It's even got a furry body. Come Ruth touch it, and you Sophia. It won't sting you. It's not alive however much it looks like a bumble bee. My father told us that the flower is doing this to attract real bees to pollinate it, so it can produce seeds. He said he had been told the bee part of the flower gives off a scent similar to what a female bumble bee gives off to attract male bumble bees.'

'I think that's really wonderful,' I said. 'And just think if Albert the farmworker hadn't spotted it and told Sophia, no one would know that this amazing bee orchid was hidden here in the midst of the grass. Perhaps there are lots of other amazing things around us that we simply don't notice.'

'I'm sure there are,' answered Mum. 'All these lovely flowers, birds, butterflies, insects, animals and trees have been created by God for his glory and our enjoyment. The Bible tells us that when Isaiah had a vision of God, the angels were singing, *Holy, holy, holy is the Lord of hosts; the whole earth is full of his glory.* [13] I'm so glad you girls have a love of nature. Do make sure that you thank God for the wonderful things he's made for us to enjoy. It will help you to learn to love him.

As I think back now, that last comment from Mum was so typical of her. She was able to see God's hand in everything and took every opportunity to direct our thoughts to him and to his word the Bible.

---

[13] Isaiah 6:3

Chapter 15

Saying Goodbye to Limden

I was fifteen. Suddenly one evening at supper, Dad astonished us all by asking: 'what would you think if we were to become sheep farmers, and live in a manor house with 500 acres of land?'

The boys were delighted at the prospect of such a change, seeing it as always, like one huge adventure. I was less enthusiastic. I had learned to love Limden Farm. It was the only home I had known and I had just begun to appreciate the chapel services at Burwash, which we attended every Sunday. We didn't have a pastor at Burwash chapel. Mum and Dad used to talk about Pastor James Weller, but he moved on in 1843 and I don't remember him at all. We had different ministers each Sunday, which as a child, I enjoyed as I felt that variety made the services more interesting. Occasionally during the preaching, I had felt a real warm, appreciative reaction to what was being said and when I thought about it, I realised this was particularly so when the preacher was talking about Jesus. Also, some of the hymns we sang moved me in a similar way. One hymn I really liked because I felt it could include me goes like this:

> When Jesus would his grace proclaim,
> He calls the simple, blind, and lame
> To come and be his guest;
> Such simple folk the world despise;

Yet simple folk have sharpest eyes,
And learn to walk the best. [14]

I felt sorry at the thought of leaving the chapel, even though I knew that Mum and Dad would ensure we found another chapel to attend wherever we lived.

I knew the last months at Limden Farm were difficult for Mum and Dad. Dad was selling off our pigs, and also reducing our herd of Sussex cattle, as well as harvesting the cereal crops including the hops. Mum was still breast feeding Dorcas who had been born in February that year, 1856, and both Elizabeth and Mary were under five years. Thankfully, we still had Ruth Parris, my cousin with us. She was three years older than me, and the two of us were made responsible for much of the routine house and dairy work.

Our new farm was at Edburton, just to the north of Brighton but separated from this seaside town by the South Downs. It was a good 30 miles from Limden Farm. We were due to move at Michaelmas, which meant that any supplies we would normally lay up in late summer and autumn to provide for the household and livestock over winter, would need to be taken with us. Dad had a good relationship with the Blaker family, the previous occupant of Perching Manor Farm and since they were effectively retiring from farming and moving to Mount Cottage, Hurstpierpoint, he was able to arrange to buy not only their sheep but also some of their winter supplies at mutually agreeable prices. Mr Blaker also allowed Dad to begin to store some of our own produce at Perching prior to the official moving date. Richard and John found themselves appointed carters that summer and made many trips across country to Edburton and back.

As the days got nearer to our move, I had to prepare myself to say farewell to my childhood home. One afternoon I found myself wandering around the farm making mental pictures of familiar scenes to take away with me and treasure.

---

[14] John Berridge 1716-1793

There, that was the spot on the river where I had seen my first otter. I had been so surprised to see the large rat-like animal amongst the reeds and then watched it slide into the water, so elegantly. Its whole shape, in particular its tail, had convinced me it was no giant rat. I had gone home and told father.

Otter

'Probably an otter,' Father had responded. 'Arthur said he had seen one the other day when we were harvesting hay in the river field.'

After that, I had seized every opportunity to sit quietly by the river near where I had seen my first otter, but although I saw water voles, moorhens and one evening to my great delight a flash of blue as a kingfisher flew swiftly upstream, it was some time before I again sighted my large, furry swimmer friend.

The next memory evoked, as I strolled on, reaching the edge of our chestnut copse, was the pleasure we had had helping Dad produce the charcoal needed each year to dry our crop of hops. The family still often spoke about old Tom Sawyer, the retired collier from Ashdown Forest, who had spent time with us over several years supervising the charcoal burns and passing on many tips from his years of experience.

In producing charcoal, it's necessary for someone to continually watch the carefully prepared rounded woodpile, where the timber was being burnt very slowly under an outer layer of wetted-down earth and turf. The moment there's any sign of flames licking up through the surface, the spot had to be quickly closed up with fresh earth and wetted down or the fire would rapidly suck in oxygen and burn far too quickly to ever produce the required charcoal.

As Richard and John had got older, Dad had commissioned them to watch the wood pile and had shown them how to close up any holes as they appeared. There was always a farm worker nearby who would come immediately if required, but by using us children as watchers Dad could give the farm worker other jobs to do.

I remembered spending an exciting night taking turns with the boys to watch the 'charcoal burn' as Dad used to refer to it. My two-hour watch had been quite scary. Most importantly, I had to be sure to stay awake, but in any case I had been far too scared to sleep. There was almost constant rustling in the fallen leaves and undergrowth around me and then an owl hooted loudly from a nearby tree. I had just convinced myself that these were all normal noises for the woodland at night, when suddenly I saw a little flame flickering on top of the charcoal burn. It took my mind only a few seconds to register that it was for this very reason I was sitting in the dark copse watching the wood pile. I needed to do something. Could I deal with this myself or should I wake Richard who was asleep in a little shelter we had built a few yards away?

I had been told clearly what to do. First I must pour a little water on the area of the earthy-turf surface where the fire was breaking through, then shovel mud from the supply that was sitting next to me in readiness for just such a situation, plonk it on the appropriate spot and pat it down hard. Could I do it? I jumped up hurriedly, but then almost fell down in a faint as a silent ghost-like presence swept past my head. It was the owl from the tree behind me. Although its hoot as it disappeared through the trees assured me it was a living creature and not a mysterious spirit, my heart continued to thump madly for some minutes.

All was well. I was able to reach the point of need, the water from my watering can quenched the flame and the mud patch I applied appeared to be holding. I put on more mud, patting it down hard and then stood back to admire my effort at first aid. The plaster was holding. Soon it would be Richard's watch and I would be able to sleep.

'*There'll be no more charcoal burning,*' I said to myself rather sadly as I wandered on. '*We won't need charcoal for sheep farming.*'

The corn crop had all been gathered in and our hop harvest completed, but it seemed sad to see no familiar haystack and all the barns nearly empty. Then I shook myself out of this melancholy. '*We are going to begin a new life on a new, bigger farm, living in a grand manor house. Come girl! Dad is convinced that God is leading us. As it was for the children of Israel of old, the pillar of cloud is moving. We must, like them, pack up our belongings and move on to new pastures, new experiences and new adventures.*'

Then another thought struck me. We are leaving little Ebenezer in the graveyard in Stonegate. But no, even that doesn't matter. That's only his body there in the ground. Little Eb is really with Jesus in heaven. I found much comfort from these thoughts and slowly made my way back to Limden farmhouse to continue helping Mum with the packing.

Part 2

My teenage years at Perching Manor Farm 1856 – 1868

Chapter 1

Michaelmas

Father took over Perching Manor Farm at Michaelmas in 1856. Being a nonconformist family, we don't have any great respect for the saint's days of the Christian calendar. However, some, such as Michaelmas, have become embedded into the culture of our country and we are happy to accept the benefits they bring by providing a structure to our year.

Perching Manor

Because at this time things were changing so rapidly in Britain through the discovery of steam power, (which had brought about the so-called industrial revolution and the exodus of so many from the countryside to the burgeoning towns and cities), I thought it would be helpful to tell you about the pattern of the year for the farming community of rural Sussex.

We have four so-called 'quarter days' which traditionally have been religious feast days and divide up the year nicely into four parts. Lady Day is the 25th March and being nine months before we celebrate the birth of Jesus, is the day to remember how the angel Gabriel appeared to Mary of Nazareth with the news that God had chosen her to be the mother of the Son of God.

The second 'quarter day' is the 24th June when we celebrate Midsummer. The pagan celebrations for midsummer take place at the Summer Solstice on the 21st June when the sun is at its highest point in the sky, but with the coming of Christianity to our island, many midsummer celebrations were moved to the Feast of John the Baptist, June 24th, which has accordingly became our second 'quarter day'.

Michaelmas, or the Feast of Michael and All Angels, September 29th, is our third 'quarter day' as it is conveniently near the autumn equinox. Christmas day on 25th December is then the fourth 'quarter day'.

These 'quarter days' have quite a significance for us as farmers. They are the days when new servants can be hired, land exchanged and debts paid. It was always father's aim, in line with general farming practice, to get the harvesting of crops fully completed by Michaelmas as this day somehow marks the end of one productive season and the beginning of a new cycle of farming.

Our move to Perching Manor Farm therefore, took place on 29th September 1856, although in reality it took several days to move our stock, farm implements and household effects across to our new location immediately north of the South Downs.

Chapter 2

Our New Home

Few things about Perching Manor have changed over the years. To this day you will find it still lying just off Edburton Lane which runs from the Shoreham to Henfield road, (to the west of us), through to Poynings and the main road south to Brighton (to our east). Although our address was Fulking, we came within the parish of Edburton and our parish church, St Andrews, was only a hundred yards or so up the lane. The parish is very proud of its church. It has a history dating back to around 940 and is said to have been founded by Edburga, the granddaughter of King Alfred the Great of Winchester. With this fact in mind, it's not hard to recognise the origin of the name of the parish.

Facing us, as we looked south was a range of hills; a range with three humps each with their own name, Edburton Hill, Perching Hill and Fulking Hill. Each little hill kept guard as it were, over its own small community. I remember feeling a particular attachment to Psalm 121 as a teenager. *'I will lift up my eyes to the hills,'* writes the Psalmist, *'from whence comes my help. My help comes from the Lord who made heaven and earth.'*

South Downs

'*Yes*', I thought to myself, '*God has given us our own hill, Perching Hill, to remind us that he is always there looking after us.*'

I found that a much more helpful thought than John's rather witty remark that we have 'Humphrey' looking over us. He had to explain to Mum, that he meant the range of South Downs in front of us with its three humps.

As you ran your eyes eastward over our hills the range rose fairly steeply to its highest peak, the Devil's Dyke. This name, however, actually belongs to the 300 feet deep, steep- sided, V-shaped valley which dropped far below the aforementioned peak of the South Downs.

As children we found the countryside surrounding our new abode full of unfamiliar yet fascinating things. It had a wealth of entirely different plant and animal habitats compared to the farm land we had been used to; we loved it. There was a tremendous amount to do when we first arrived so it wasn't until the following spring that we could more fully appreciate the surrounding countryside.

Being the oldest girl, then 15 years, I was expected to be Mother's chief helper. Thinking back, Mum truly worked miracles in the way she looked after ten children, ran the house and gave Dad the support he needed, both on the farm and with his increasing number of preaching engagements. All of us children had our jobs to do, but it was my responsibility to organise the younger girls and to show them how to play their part in the home.

I loved to get out on the Downs as much as possible and an excellent excuse to do this was the need to exercise the dog we had then. She was a small fox terrier named Jessie. Fox terriers have the reputation of being excellent rat catchers. Since Dad was adamant that all of us, including our animals, had a purpose and played a useful part in the running of our home and farm, killing rats was Jessie's reason for being. She lived outside in her kennel and although mostly had the run of the farmyard, she still loved a walk on the Downs with me.

Our South Downs presented a completely open landscape, uncluttered by fences, hedges or stone walls and even trees are quite rare. Sheep grazed this pasture land under the watchful eye of their shepherd and his dog. Sheep farming was a new experience for father when we first came, but George Payne who had served the Blakers before us at Perching Manor as shepherd, had been glad to stay on, and father depended on his knowledge and expertise constantly in those early days.

The thumb rule at that time, on our pasture land, was one sheep per acre, so father aimed to maintain a flock of up to 500 ewes. The form of shepherding we used was known as 'folding', which incidentally, must have been very similar to shepherding as the Bible portrays. At night the sheep are kept in an enclosure, or fold, then at dawn the shepherd with his dog led the flock out onto the hillside, watched over them all day and brought them back to the fold at dusk. By enclosing the sheep at night on areas of arable land, as much as this is possible, helped to fertilise the soil and benefit the crops.

Chapter 3

Skylarks

I loved talking to George or Mr Payne as I used to call him. Spending his days on the hillside, he was so knowledgeable about many aspects of the Sussex Downs and was always delighted to share this knowledge with anyone patient enough to listen.

It was a sunny day in May. I had managed to escape from the never-ending chores in the house, had whistled Jessie and together we had set off to climb Perching Hill. Jessie had learned from bitter experience that she mustn't chase sheep, so after an initial run around on the lower slopes, as we got higher and approached grazing ewes with their lambs skipping around, she kept fairly close to me.

'Please, Mr Payne,' I began, that particular day, 'can you tell me about the skylarks, there are far more here than we had at Limden Farm and they seem to be able to sing all day?'

'Yes, larks are one of my favourite birds,' my shepherd friend replied. 'Look at that little fellow there, soaring heavenward singing his very heart out. I've sometimes thought they are angels in disguise, putting us mortals to shame in the way they sing praise to their maker all day long. But you know Ruth, as I've watched them I've realised something that's not so obvious to a casual listener. That little lark will only sing for three or four minutes, I guess that's all his tiny throat and lungs can sustain. Look he's already sinking back onto the hillside.

But then listen over there, another is taking his place. The thing is we have so many larks on these Sussex Downs that on a day like this, their song is almost continuous even though one little bird can only sing for a few minutes. If you think about it, that's a lesson for us in our worship and service for God.'

Skylark

'At school, Mr Payne, I interjected at this point, 'we learned a poem by Shelley about skylarks:

Hail to thee, blithe Spirit!
Bird thou never wert,
That from Heaven, or near it,
Pourest thy full heart
In profuse strains of unpremeditated art.

Higher still and higher
From the earth thou springest
Like a cloud of fire;
The blue deep thou wingest,
And singing still dost soar, and soaring ever singest.

In the golden lightning
Of the sunken sun,
O'er which clouds are bright'ning,
Thou dost float and run;
Like an unbodied joy whose race is just begun.

The pale purple even
Melts around thy flight;
Like a star of Heaven,
In the broad day-light
Thou art unseen, but yet I hear thy shrill delight,'

Percy Bysshe Shelley 1792–1822

'That's beautiful, Ruth,' said George, 'can you say it again so I can get my head around it. How I wish I could read and enjoy poetry!'

'I'm afraid I don't know much poetry,' I confessed, 'but our teacher at Stonegate school, Miss Read, loved poems about nature and that was one she made us repeat until we knew it by heart.

'Another thing of interest Mr Payne,' I added with a smile, 'the poet Shelley spent his childhood in Sussex. His family's home was near Horsham I'm told, so perhaps he wrote that lovely poem whilst walking here on our South Downs, You never know.'

I think I should however add one other less savoury comment about the larks. We enjoyed their song tremendously, but often in autumn these little songsters flocked down to us from further north in their thousands and become a real curse to the farmers, devouring the early tender shoots of freshly sown wheat. In the years when this has happened, father arranged for our men to net them, as he'd discovered there was quite a market for them amongst the higher class poulterers in Brighton, who then sold them trussed and ready for roasting.

Chapter 4

Blue Butterflies and Dangerous Snakes

I have warm memories of both the many walks on our local hillside and the interesting chats I had with George Payne. One particular encounter with our shepherd stands out above the others.

It was late summer, harvest was just over and I had grasped one of those rare opportunities to get away from the farm by myself. Often Mother persuaded me to take the younger girls when I walked Jessie on the hillside, but that day, I had left my sisters churning butter and had set off in a cheerful mood. Being by myself, gave me the chance to talk aloud to God and I have always found I can concentrate on my prayers more easily this way. Often my prayers led me into song and all this just wasn't possible with an entourage of sisters in tow.

The afternoon was still and rather sultry; all nature seemed to be asleep. The larks were quiet. There were a few butterflies flitting around but even they seemed only half-hearted in the pursuit of whatever they feed on in the downland vegetation. I really love our little Chalk Hill Blue butterfly. Some summers there are so many fluttering at a low level across the grassland, that they create a beautiful blue shimmering effect. It's only the male butterfly that is blue, the female being brown, but both have the same patterned border around the edge of their wings.

Father had always encouraged us in our love of nature and both to further our education and ensure we had worthwhile conversations in the evenings, he used to challenge us older children to gather information about subjects of our choice, to converse meaningfully with the rest of the family. One month, I chose the Chalk Hill Blue butterfly and have discovered that understanding more about specific aspects of God's wonderful creation, adds tremendously to the enjoyment of country walks.

The habitat of my favourite little blue butterfly is restricted to hillsides where Horseshoe Vetch grows, simply because this is the plant that their larvae feed on. It is a lovely yellow variety of vetch but it only grows on chalk, hence the Chalk Hill Blue butterfly as its name implies, is confined to chalk hills like our South Downs.

The butterflies are to be seen in July and August and their main purpose at that point is to propagate. The shimmering waves of blue, seen occasionally on sunny summer days are flocks of rapacious males searching for females to mate with.

Although each small larva develops within the egg during the late summer and autumn, it doesn't emerge to feed on the Horseshoe Vetch leaves until the warmer weather around Easter of the following year. The larvae are night-time feeders, eating away the underside of the vetch leaves beneath the security of darkness, then hiding themselves during the hours of daylight. Throughout June, they are in the chrysalis stage and the mature butterflies emerge in early July when their life cycle begins all over again.

During the summer, over several evenings, as soon as darkness fell, I did this research into the life of my favourite blue butterfly. I crept up the hillside with a lantern to discover for myself what their caterpillars looked like. I was overjoyed to locate some feeding on clumps of vetch and can confirm that they have a green somewhat-hairy body with two yellow lines down their back and an additional yellow line just above each row of tiny feet.

Still, I must come back to that particular afternoon's walk.

As I made my way steadily up the hill with Jessie running madly around, obviously discovering many wonderful smells requiring her urgent attention, I realised we would soon be getting near the sheep and I would need to call my companion to heel, and proceed more carefully.

'Whatever is George doing?' I asked myself, catching sight of father's shepherd bending over the body of one of our sheep.

'Don't look Ruth!' George cried. 'You've just come at the wrong moment.'

'Why, Mr Payne?' I responded. 'What's happened?'

At that point I realised what the shepherd was doing. With the sharp knife that he always carried in a sheath on his belt, and a small saw, he was in the process of decapitating one of our lambs. Being now nearly five months old, the animal was a good size and the process was proving quite a task.

I waited until the shepherd had completely removed the head of the lamb and then looked towards him expectantly. All sorts of thoughts had gone through my mind and I really couldn't see any reason for what he was doing.

'Ruth,' he said, 'I'm saving the animals life.' Such a comment served only to confuse me further.

'This poor creature was bitten in the mouth by an adder, Mr Payne explained. 'I witnessed the animal's distress from a distance and knew at once what had happened. The result of such a bite is usually death for a sheep but it's not the snake's poison that normally kills it, but the fact that the poor animal's nose swells up, stopping her breathing so that she suffocates. It's now standard procedure on the South Downs here, to quickly kill snake-bitten sheep and to cut off their heads before the poison can get too far into the bloodstream. The lamb's meat is then fit to eat and so we haven't in fact lost an animal. That's what I meant by saying I was saving its life. Your mother will be pleased to have a lamb to feed the family for a couple of days, so there's not a lot of financial loss for your father. And,' he added with a satisfied smile, 'I'm hoping he'll give a good joint to my wife for the family, which is customary in these circumstances.'

'What family do you have Mr Payne?' I asked inquisitively. 'I've seen you often with a boy helping you. Is he one of your children?'

'Yes, that's my eldest boy, George,' answered Mr Payne proudly, rubbing his bloody hands on the grass. 'He's learning to be a shepherd like his dad. Then I have two daughters, Ann and Mary, and another two younger sons, Charles and Friend.'

'Friend' seemed a very strange name to give a child but I didn't like to comment so with a smile I answered, 'I'll certainly make sure you get a good chunk of lamb's meat Mr Payne. It'll be a real treat for your family. I'm sure you deserve it,' I added grinning, 'you saved the life of that healthy-looking lamb just in the nick of time'

I could see that Jessie was getting impatient to continue her walk. She had been very good sitting at my feet and I didn't want to overstretch this test of her obedience, but I had one further question for my shepherd friend.

'Are there many snakes here on the hillside?' I asked.

'Adders are the only dangerous ones,' Mr Payne replied. 'I kill them if I see them and some years there seem to be more than others. A lad on a neighbouring farm was bitten last summer. He had put his hand down a rabbit hole thinking there might be a wheatear's nest there when an adder bit him. He survived but they say one side of his body went black and blue and he was quite ill for a while with a horrible nausea.'

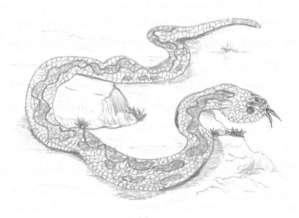

Adder

'Whoa, that's awful,' I said shuddering. 'But aren't there friendly snakes too?'

'Grass snakes are fairly common,' answered Mr Payne. 'They are easily recognisable as they haven't got those V shapes down their back like adders have. They are quite harmless and yet grow bigger than any deadly adder.'

'My brother came home from the fields with a slow worm in his pocket the other week,' I commented. 'It looked like a snake, but father had told Richard it was quite harmless.'

'Yes,' responded George, 'slow worms are very attractive, but their name is rather daft as they are neither slow nor worms. Some people call them blind worms, but that's also misleading as they do have eyes to see with; the ordinary earthworm lacks eyesight. You sometimes see slow worms without a tail though; their back quarters look very stunted.'

'Dad, told us about that,' I answered. 'He said that God had given them the ability to release their tail from their body as a means of protection when attacked. The tail remains wriggling in front of the confused predator while the slow worm itself escapes.'

I enjoyed my conversations with George Payne. He was a kind, considerate man. Spending each day on the hillside with mostly just his sheep and dog for company, I found him eager to chat and share his knowledge of the countryside, much of which he'd simply picked up through his own observation and life experience.

Chapter 5

The Vision

It was during those early days at Perching Manor that I had what I like to refer to as 'my vision'. It was something very personal staying with me all my life although the details have become somewhat refined, as my understanding of the Bible has grown. Because it was so precious to me, for years I wasn't willing to speak of it to anyone as it would have hurt me very much to have had it critically analysed and perhaps mocked. Eventually after my marriage, I felt able to talk about it to my husband. Vision is maybe the wrong term. It is an imaginary sequence of pictures in my mind, which started in a fairly simple form and then over time, developed as new thoughts emerged. My husband suggested it was simply the way my mind was able to grasp and remember things that were important to me.

As I've thought about it in order to write this, I believe the seed of my vision must have been sown in my very early childhood, probably at my mother's knee, when she would tell us in simple terms about God and what the Bible says about him. The picture of God that I took away with me as a young child was of a happy family. I'm sure the word 'family' to describe the Godhead, was not one used either by my mother or of by any of our preachers, but I so loved the thought that God was three persons in one, bound together in love and perfect harmony of mind and purpose, that in my childish mind I viewed this as the perfect family. Maybe my fascination with such an idea, developed as being contrary to the background of angry voices sometimes raised within our own home. There certainly were times when I became quite frightened by father's discipline of my older brothers. To hear that within the Godhead family, Father and Son never had a disagreement but just enjoyed loving each other, thrilled me as a little girl.

I remember, when much younger, I would often close my eyes and think about God and what I liked to call my vision, was made up of the different scenes in my imagination. Some aspects of God thrilled me, but it would equally be true to say, others worried me considerably.

Expressing these scenes in words is not so easy but I will try to envisage some of them afresh and share them with you.

In the first scene the setting is, as the Bible describes it, 'in the beginning'. I 'saw' the triune God, namely this loving 'family', Father, Son and Holy Spirit, in conference. They were planning to create the world. The persons of the Godhead had no physical form, as they are purely spirit but they now purposed to create a material universe full of stars and a wonderful earth which would be the home of physical beings, endowed with the spiritual capacity to commune with God.

But there was an enemy. God was served by many lower spiritual beings called angels whom he had created. The majority of these were completely holy and happy serving God with delight but at some point, one of them, named Lucifer or Satan, had rebelled. He had been able to rally a proportion of his fellow angels to support him and had set himself against God. This had caused God to expel these fallen angels from his presence.

'What if Satan persuades the 'humans' we are making, to rebel against us and follow him?' asked the Son of God.

'He will do that and he will succeed,' answered the Father. 'Adam, the man we are planning to make, must have the option of choosing whom he will serve. Satan is powerful and very subtle and I know he will tempt Adam and his wife to disobey me. I know they will fall and come under his power and control.'

'If we know that, why are we creating them?' asked the third person of the Godhead.

'It will bring great glory to us and reveal another aspect of our divine character in forgiving them,' answered the Father.

'But our righteousness won't allow us to simply forgive sin,' commented the Son of God.

'What do you suggest we do?' asked the Father.

There was silence for a while and then the Son of God responded. 'If we love them enough, I could become a human and bear their punishment for them.'

'Yes, we do love them enough,' answered the Father, 'but it will mean much physical and spiritual suffering. To pay the price of human sin you must endure my curse, die and be cut off from my love until the full price is paid.'

There was another silence and then the Son of God said, 'but will that be enough to win them back from Satan's power? I would want them to respond voluntarily to my death for them.'

'In and of itself your suffering for them won't be enough,' answered the Father. 'Satan's power is strong and he won't release them willingly. Sin will have killed their spiritual capacity to respond to our love. Many must die eternally to demonstrate how serious sin is, but the offer of eternal life must be available for all and those who respond to it will be saved'.

'I can see that it will be my work to convince them of their sin, to reveal our love and to draw them into saving faith,' said the Holy Spirit quietly.

'It will not be everyone,' added the Father. 'I already know who they are. It is a vast number and I will give them to you my Son. At the time I appoint, we will give you a human body; you will need to suffer much but you will have such joy. All those I give you, will, through the powerful influence of the Holy Spirit, respond to our love and be yours in a love relationship for all eternity.

So was the first scene of my 'vision'. It was based initially on the truth I learned at my mother's knee with other details added as I read the Bible for myself and listened to our preachers. It has had a tremendous influence on me all my life.

I want to tell you one more scene. Man had now been on the earth about two thousand years. All had happened as God had pre-ordained and foreseen, indeed, the triune God was now preparing the way for the entrance of the Son of God into a world alienated from their Creator through wilful disobedience. God had set his love on a man named Abraham. He had spoken to this man in an unmistakable way and the Holy Spirit had moved Abraham to believe, trust and obey the voice of God. This faith and obedience had necessitated Abraham to leave his family home, the worship of his family's gods and together with his wife and possessions, to become a nomad wandering under God's guidance towards a new promised country. God promised Abraham great blessing and he would father a family, in particular a son through whom mankind would be blessed.

All this was the background to a particular experience Abraham had, which so stirred my imagination it became far more to me than merely another incident in his life story. It was so tangible; in my imagination I felt I was actually present when it occurred.

One night God had called Abraham out of his tent. 'Look at the sky,' God said. 'Admire those stars'.

In the clear, still air of that desert-like location, free of any artificial light, the night sky was awe-inspiring.

'Can you count those stars?' asked God.

Realising that it was hopeless to try, Abraham had to reply in the negative. 'They are breath-taking,' he answered, 'and far, far too many for me to number.'

'They represent the family I'm going to give you,' said God.

I learned the meaning of that vision through comments my father made when reading the story from Genesis, at our supper table.

Dad told us that Jesus, the Christ, the Son of God, was the promised 'seed of Abraham' through whom the whole world was to be blessed. The stars, he said, which represent the children of Abraham, are God's elect. They are the innumerable men, women and children out of every nation who have the same faith as 'father' Abraham.

These are not necessarily the natural seed of Abraham, but all those who belong to Abraham's son Jesus through faith in him.

I quickly realised that these were those referred to in my first 'vision', those whom the Father gave to the Son before the world was created. For many years what worried me considerably was the vital question: 'Am I one of those stars?'

Chapter 6

Religious Neighbours

O ur family's social status as farmers, living in Perching Manor and employing about twenty workers, (men, boys and women), made it difficult to relate to the village folk around us. Also, father's position, as a nonconformist minister, added to the gulf that separated us. I know mother felt this keenly. She would sometimes comment that it was so difficult to really get alongside our neighbours. When she knew of illness or family problems in the village, she would call by with a jar of jam or honey to show sympathy and would be so frustrated that our neighbours, many of whom were our employees, wouldn't or couldn't talk to her at a level which enabled her to really help them.

It was also the pressure of these social distinctions, which was the biggest reason for my parents' decision to send my younger sisters away to boarding school, rather than to the village church school. I know it was a great relief to my mother when they discovered that one of Dad's cousins in Brighton ran a small school and was able to take the younger children as pupil boarders. The girls were relatively happy with our cousin Eliza, and we were often able to fetch them home for the weekend.

One day at supper, father announced that he had met a very interesting farming family whom he felt it would be possible to nurture friendship with.

'Tell us about them Eli,' asked my mother expressing great interest. 'Who are they and where do they live?'

'Their name is Robinson, and they are farming about 900 acres at Saddlescombe Farm which is tucked away on the slopes of the Downs just south of Poynings,' answered my father.

'Oh, Saddlescombe farm,' I said. 'Our butcher from Henfield goes on to deliver to the Robinson family at Saddlescombe. I don't know exactly where it is but he says they are good customers.'

'What were you doing chatting to that butcher's boy?' murmured my brother John with a mischievous grin.

Thankfully my parents' didn't hear John's comment, and I didn't need to defend myself. Ignoring my brother, I looked across to my father for more information.

'Yes, I met Martin Robinson at the sheep fair and we had a very interesting conversation,' he continued. 'One of the members of the Baptist chapel in Poynings works for him and had spoken about us here in Perching adding the fact I was an Independent minister. The Robinson family are Quakers and from what I could gather, hold very devout Christian principles.'

'Whatever are Quakers?' asked my brother Richard.

'This is the first Quaker family I've met personally,' answered father,' and I guess as in most Christian denominations, there are some formal legalistic members as well as some truly heart-changed believers in Jesus. That said I understand that the basis of the Quaker's Christian belief is biblical and evangelical, but it's their form of worship that is strange to us. The emphasis is on quietness and sitting still before God in personal, reflective worship. Occasionally someone, either man or woman, will speak, but this should only happen if they sense the Holy Spirit is moving and inspiring them. On some occasions, I'm given to understand, the whole service of an hour or so will pass in complete silence.'

'Wouldn't that leave them open to false teaching and human ideas which aren't biblical?' asked mother, with a worried frown.

'That's my fear too,' responded father.

'However it must be said, the Quaker believers have had some positive influence on society in our country and I understand the Robinson family are well respected by their employees, even though they don't allow either harvest suppers or the drinking of alcohol.'

'Where do the Robinsons worship?' I asked. 'Where is the nearest Quaker church?'

'They call their buildings "Meeting Houses" rather than churches,' answered father, 'I believe the Robinsons attend one in Ship Street, Brighton.'

The conversation about Quakers went on for some time and then father made the point on which he had started the conversation.

'Mr Robinson very kindly suggested that he would like us to meet his wife and children,' Dad ventured to say, 'and I was wondering, Seli, whether you might find time to call by with our children? I believe the Robinson children are somewhat younger than our older ones. From what Martin said, their oldest, Emily, was born the same year as little Ebenezer.'

As I've mentioned before, Ebenezer was the little brother we lost when he was just thirteen months old. I remember well the day we buried him in the Stonegate Church graveyard near Limden Farm. I found it very telling that father still identified the year 1848 as the year of Ebenezer's birth.

'I'd like to come with you, Mum,' I said eagerly. 'We could take the younger ones to meet the Robinson children.'

Chapter 7

Saddlescombe Farm

It was an April afternoon when we first visited Saddlescombe Farm; I believe the year was 1858. Mum drove the pony and trap and I looked after three of my sisters in the back. Mother had decided that we shouldn't swamp Mrs Robinson's farmhouse with children, so we had only brought Naomi, aged eleven, Mercy, aged eight and Mary aged six. We didn't have many outings, apart from chapel on Sundays, so the girls were very excited.

Our drive took us through Fulking village and on eastwards into Poynings, where we took the little lane south up onto the slopes of the Downs where Saddlescombe Farm was situated. Mum had chosen a dry, sunny day for our outing, although isolated clouds where moving fairly quickly across the lovely blue sky occasionally obscuring the sun for a few minutes.

We had not been able to warn Mrs Robinson of our visit, so we hoped it would not be an inconvenient afternoon for her.

The farmhouse was very similar in size and design to Perching Manor. As a low brick wall separated the house from the lane, it was plain to see there was no obvious sign of activity as we drove up to the front of the house. No front gate merely a wide opening in the wall allowed access to the front door.

'Perhaps you'll go and knock on the door and introduce us to the maid, Ruth,' suggested mother. 'I'll look after the girls and only bring them in, if it's convenient.'

A maidservant about my own age, who I later learned had the rather attractive name of Priscilla, opened the door. I explained we were the Page family from Perching Manor Farm and hoped Mrs Robinson was at home and willing to receive us.

'It's really lovely that you've come,' exclaimed Mrs Robinson enthusiastically, as she came to greet us in the large front drawing room into which Priscilla had ushered us. 'We don't get many visitors as you can well imagine, and my husband mentioned that he had met this interesting neighbouring farmer with the lovely biblical name of Eli.'

'Yes, I'm Eli Page's wife Selina, and these are some of our daughters, Ruth, Naomi, Mercy and Mary,' responded mother.

Mrs Robinson looked at us four girls and commented with some astonishment, 'just some of your daughters, Mrs Page. How many more have you got?'

Mother looked a little embarrassed but answered with a hint of pride, 'Eli and I have four more daughters and three sons.'

'I really must congratulate you my dear lady,' responded Mrs Robinson. 'God has really blessed you and I must say you still look so young and healthy as do the children of course.'

'Yes, God has been good to us,' answered mother. 'We've only lost one little boy and all my children are indeed healthy and strong. As I'm sure you will agree a well-run farm is a very healthy environment in which to bring up children.'

Mrs Robinson nodded in agreement then after a few moments of comfortable silence she commented, 'the history behind our farm is extremely interesting; I'll tell you about it over a cup of tea, if you have time to stay a while. But I guess the girls would like to the meet our children. Emily is my eldest and she's just ten years old. Then we have two sons, Charles[1] and Frank, two daughters, Bertha and Ada, and our youngest is Earnest, he is just two years old. I'll call Emily and she

---

[1] Charles was away at Bailey Hall, School, Hertforshire in 1861

can show your girls around the farmyard and I'm sure they would like to see our rather special well.'

Later that day at supper, mother was eager to tell all of us what she had learned about the Robinson's farm. In the following account, I have added a few more facts which I have discovered since.

Saddlescombe Farm had a long history. After the conquest of Britain by William the Conquerer in 1066, the new king commissioned a survey of his domain to determine from every landowner the extent and value of the land and livestock. This was completed in 1089 and became known as the Domesday Book. In it, the hamlet of Saddlescombe was referred to as 'Selscombe'. It was essentially a manor house and farmland, and in 1225 this was granted to an order of soldier monks known as the Knights Templar. A little later during the reign of Edward II, (1307-1327) the reputation of the Knights of Templar worsened to such an extent that the order was dissolved by Pope John XXII and Saddlescombe Manor was given over to the Knights of St John.

It was the work of these knights from that period, which had left Saddlescombe with its most significant feature. A deep well, dug about 150 feet deep, through layers of chalk to a source of fresh underground water. In order to draw water, a large wooden wheel was constructed. A massive oak beam formed the axle of the wheel on which was attached a single chain with a large, wooden, iron-bound bucket at each end. These buckets held about 12 gallons of water, and as the wheel turned, one went down the well as the other came up full of water. The wheel was driven by a donkey or pony walking around inside it, like a mouse in a cage.

Emily took the younger girls and me to see the treadwheel, housed in a square wooden shed, open on one side. One of the

Saddlescombe Wheelhouse,

farm workers took very little persuasion to set the wheel working. He
fetched an old white donkey named Smoker from a nearby paddock
and since drawing water had been his job for longer than anyone
can remember, he knew exactly what to do. He walked without any
hesitation into the wheel and then treading steadily forward, he slowly
caused the wheel to turn as he walked. Up came a bucketful of water
and we were offered a cup of it to taste. It was clear, cold and delicious.

Chapter 8

Getting to Know Father

Most Thursday evenings, father would travel across to Henfield, to preach to a small group of believers there. I heard him tell mother that they met in a small cottage and the friends who gathered, were very keen to hear the word of God. Their obvious appreciation of his interest in them, and his preaching, convinced him that this was indeed a calling from God.

It suddenly occurred to me that I could go with him. I didn't want to give the impression that my interest was spiritual, in fact at that point, I don't think it was. I just thought it would be rather fun to ride with father in the pony and trap, giving me a change of scene and a chance to meet some interesting new people, perhaps even an attractive young man. Father had also talked about the friends' generosity in providing a good tea with home-made Victoria sponge cake. Anyway, I tentatively suggested to Mum I would be interested in going with father occasionally, if she could spare me at home. Thinking back now, I realise I could have suggested Mum went herself with father sometimes and I could take responsibility for the children, but I'm afraid that never crossed my mind.

Mum's main concern was that I would be very late home as Father would often stay and talk and his pastoral care of the families at Henfield, he felt was an integral part of his ministry there. However,

we all knew that a post coach came along Edburton Lane, past
Perching Farm on the way to Poynings and Brighton most evenings
and father suddenly realised it probably came via Henfield. The next
day he stopped the driver and asked whether this was actually true,
if so, whether it would be possible for him to bring me back on a
Thursday evening. All was agreed, so it soon became a regular part of
my week to travel across to Henfield with father, have tea with one of
the families there, attend the cottage meeting and then return home
by post coach.

Most weeks we were entertained to tea by Isaac and Ann Woolgar
who ran a market garden with their son Stephen on Henfield
Common. Stephen wasn't married but since he was a lot older than
me, I was saved from looking on him as a possible husband. However
Isaac and Ann had another son Henry, whose wife Elizabeth came
from the neighbouring village of Albourne. I think she must have
talked about me to friends in Albourne because, after I had been going
with father for some time, a young man about my own age, from
there, began to join the meeting from time to time. I'll tell you more
about him later.

Riding regularly with father those five miles to Henfield each
week, taught me to really appreciate him and I'm pretty certain I can
say, I got closer to him than any of my brothers or sisters ever did.

To me, father seemed to know everything there was to know
about the countryside, and sometimes he would also talk to me about
the Bible text that he believed God had given him to preach on that
evening. On other occasions, he would say to me, 'Ruth, my dear,
today I need to just pray and think, so if you see anything interesting
as we drive, just keep it in mind to tell me later.'

One afternoon in particular stands out in my mind. It was early
summer and the men were mowing hay as we left Perching. I had a
good knowledge of the commoner birds around on the South Downs,
but that day the bird that we saw flitting in front of us looked rather
unusual. When it settled on a gate post a little ahead of us, father
halted the pony and we were able to see it more clearly. It was bigger
than a sparrow or a robin, but perhaps not quite as big as a starling. It

had a white breast and its head was also whitish. Its back was reddish brown but clearly evident, was a thick black line across the face and through its eye.

Red-backed Shrike

'Look at that now!' said father. 'It's a few years since I've seen one of those. That's a red-backed shrike. When I was a lad we saw them quite regularly on our farm in Hellingly. They've got a very unusual habit which has given them the nickname of 'butcher birds'. They feed on large insects, lizards, frogs and even small birds and once they've had enough to eat, they will begin to stock up a larder, piercing the creatures they catch on thorns in the hedgerow.

'Look there it goes. See, its tail has a black and white pattern similar to that of a wheatear. That bird was a male. The female is less distinctive with more brown on her.'

I was thrilled to see my first red-backed shrike and couldn't wait to tell my brothers about it. Father, too, was excited about seeing this beautiful bird so clearly on the gate post. It obviously gave him new thoughts for his sermon and because I felt I had shared in the preparation for it, I listened more carefully than sometimes and was quite disappointed when I had to leave early to catch my coach home. Incidentally, because I couldn't see a clock, it was father's habit to look across to me at the appropriate time and say: 'right girl, it's time for you to be going.' This used to embarrass me at first, but very soon all of us got used to it, and the friends would nod and smile at me as I left.

Father took for his text that evening the words in Luke chapter 2 verse 51, where it says of Mary the mother of Jesus that she '*kept all these sayings in her heart*'. Amongst the thoughts he brought to us from this text was the following: when the Holy Spirit brings the word of God alive to us, there is usually far more than we can take in at one sitting. 'Don't lose out on the blessings that may still be there to nourish your soul,' he said. 'The red-backed shrike stores excess food on thorns in the hedgerow; we need to keep God's word active in our minds and hearts by meditating on it, praying over it. We will then often find there is a store of food in those words of Scripture to last us for days.'

Spending time alone with father also gave me the opportunity to ask him about things I didn't understand. I was very hesitant to ask him about spiritual things because in some obtuse way, I felt to give the impression I was interested would make me a hypocrite. There was however a text that really worried me. In a Scripture reading at supper one evening, the words *Many are called but few are chosen* had come like a thunderbolt from heaven, shattering my complacency and sending me to bed with a renewed, nagging fear I was eternally lost. Surely these words of Jesus must mean if God hadn't chosen me, I could never have a conversion experience or never become one of his favoured people, who I envied so much.

I was so glad that I did manage to tentatively ask father what that Scripture actually meant. It was such a relief to find his answer didn't condemn me completely, or leave me dependant on what one might call fate.

'Ruth,' father said, looking at me earnestly, 'all Scripture is saying actually fits in exactly with what experience shows us. This verse is simply explaining what everyone knows happens. Think about it. Many hear the gospel message. The life of Jesus and many of his teachings are widely understood. Millions of people around the world celebrate Christmas and sing about the birth of the Saviour of mankind. Millions celebrate Easter and know Jesus of Nazareth died on a Roman cross, was buried and the Bible teaches he defeated death and came back to life again. All this is widely known. It's not a secret whispered about behind closed church doors. But hearing and knowing these essential details about Jesus, as they are related to us in the New Testament Gospels, demand a response. Jesus' preaching, in a nutshell, is summarised for us in Mark's Gospel as "*Repent and come follow me.*" Therefore, whether people realise it or not, the Christian message is a call. "*Many are called.*" But how many feel the power of this call in their hearts and consciences? How many respond to it?

Experience shows us it is but few. In Jesus' own day there were but few who became his genuine followers and this has been the same down through the centuries. There have always been many superficial followers, but their lack of sincerity is revealed when things get difficult and their faith is tested.

'Genuine followers of Jesus have only become such, because God has put new spiritual life within them and the Bible describes them as God's chosen ones. But no one need think this excludes them. The Bible constantly repeats God's promise, if we seek we shall find and no one who sincerely seeks for mercy, will be turned away.

'Remember that, Ruth my girl,' added father. 'Don't let that verse depress you. Although Jesus said "*few are chosen*", he also said "*whosoever will, may come*". Today is still the day of salvation. Seek for mercy while you can and I can assure you if you are serious in this and persevere, then on the authority of Scripture, God will show you great and mighty things and reveal to you the joy of his salvation.'

Chapter 9

My Parents Reminisce

Listening to mother and father reminisce was always enjoyable. It didn't happen all that often but when it did, I felt it enabled me to understand more of the world around me and of people I only knew by name, but in many cases, had influenced the lives of my parents.

Father often referred to different preachers whose ministry had been a real blessing to him and by the early 1860s several of them had passed on to glory. Mr William Crouch had been pastor at Pell Green, near Wadhurst. The early 1800s were years when God was raising up many village nonconformist fellowships. On feeling a burden to share the word of God he so loved, William Crouch began to hold meetings for about a dozen villagers in the kitchen of a carpenter friend, Thomas Kemp. In 1818 he baptised nine candidates and a church membership was formed. As numbers increased, Mr Kemp graciously gave a plot of land for a chapel and erected the building largely at his own expense. The Holy Spirit was moving in the village and the surrounding area so very soon, more conversions necessitated a more spacious meeting place. The chapel was enlarged three times, in 1828, 1831 and 1841. Since the earliest chapel had no baptistery, a pond behind Pell Farm House was used to baptise converts.

I loved to hear these accounts of God working in the villages of
Sussex and I remembered Dad saying William Crouch had been pastor
in Pell Green for 45 years. Dad went to his funeral in February 1861.
One day towards the end of his life, Mr Crouch had been travelling
home from a preaching engagement at Ninfield when a wheel from his
conveyance came off, throwing him heavily onto the ground. He lost
consciousness and it was later discovered that a bone in his arm was
broken. He was then 71 years old and he never really recovered. He
preached on three more Sundays and on January 20th twice, his text
at both services being *But be filled with the Spirit* Eph. 5:18. During
the evening service, he appeared unable to speak for a few minutes and
later said it was as though something moved inside him. He felt so full
of the love of God he could summon no words to adequately express
it. This was his last sermon. The following Saturday evening his son
Jacob came to see him, when he asked his father if he knew him, the
answer was 'Yes Jacob. I am a true Jacob, bowed down with old age,
but blessed of my God'.

William Crouch passed on to glory on Monday 4th February 1861.
Shortly before his final breath, he was heard to exclaim with the glow
of heaven on his face, 'the golden gates, the golden gates, the golden
gates!'[2]

Four months later, father attended the funeral of William Cowper
at the Dicker. That evening, at supper, Mum and Dad talked excitedly
about Mr Cowper and I realised it was at a service they had both
attended, (before they were married), when William Cowper had been
preaching, father had found the joy of the assurance of his salvation.

'Do you remember Seli,' asked my father, with a beam on his face,
'that when we came out of the Dicker chapel that afternoon, I said I
was now ready to die?'

'I remember all too well, Eli,' answered mother, 'but I also
remember my reply, hoping it wouldn't be just yet because I still
needed you. Then I added something which proved to be rather

---

[2] S. F. Paul; Further History of Gospel Standard Baptists, Vol 2 pp 43-46

prophetic. I said perhaps God wanted to leave you here to tell others about his love for poor sinners in Jesus Christ.'

As I listened to this conversation, I felt such a deep longing inside me that I could hardly bear it. When would God hear my prayers and give me such assurance that I was his child?

When I could settle my mind again I realised father was telling mother a bit more about William Cowper.

Just to avoid confusion, this was not the same William Cowper who wrote some of those lovely hymns we sing. The latter had been a contemporary of John Newton and had died in the previous century.

William Cowper of Sussex rather, had been a very earnest and powerful preacher. He was a convinced Baptist at a period when, like my parents many nonconformist Calvinists were influenced by William Huntington and saw no need for believer's baptism. Father said that his sermons were often very cutting and condemning. He preached a righteous, holy God whose laws condemned the whole human race to eternal damnation. However, as father himself had experienced, having left his hearers with no grounds for self-satisfaction, he then showed there was mercy through Jesus Christ, for all who in repentance, embraced God's Son as their Saviour.

Zoar Chapel at the Dicker, flourished under his pastoral care for twenty years but in God's mysterious providence, William Cowper had some form of stroke in 1857 which impaired his memory and eventually left him unable to read. For the next four years, he continued to preach from time to time as God enabled him, but he was a shadow of his former self and occasionally, gave the impression he had even forgotten the text he was preaching from. A final stroke in the June of 1861 entirely paralysed him and he died quietly that same month. [3]

A further funeral the following year was that of Thomas Pitcher. He had been a blacksmith in Hellingly, who on experiencing the power of God's Spirit in his life, had felt a burden to preach. Having discovered salvation was not through religious activity or a ritualistic

---

[3] S. F. Paul; Further History of the Gospel Standard Baptists, Vol 2 pp 58-60

form of worship, but simply through grace alone, in trusting the finished work of Jesus Christ on his behalf, he felt God's call to share that message. The village of Hellingly near the Dicker, had been my father's childhood home and Thomas Pitcher had been the minister of the small independent chapel there during those years. Interestingly, I remember my parents saying Mr Pitcher had asked the local vicar from the Anglican Church to take his funeral as he had a good relationship with him. However, there was a further memorial service at Zoar Chapel, Dicker, when Mr John Grace preached the sermon.[4]

'Eli,' said my mother with a smile, 'you will surely remember that it was at an anniversary service at the Hellingly chapel, when you asked me to walk out with you for the first time?'

'Yes, answered my father, 'and you wouldn't give me an answer.'

'How could I agree to be your girl when everyone knew you were the ringleader of all the rowdy youths in the village? sighed my mother. I remember saying to myself, '*Why does it have to be Eli Page asking me out for my first date?*'

This was the first time I had heard such a story and was obviously eager to hear more, but all father said by way of answer was: 'Seli, my darling, I believe it was your prayers and gentle influence, together with the death of my dear father, that brought me to my knees seeking God's mercy.' [5]

---

[4] Ralph Chambers: Strict Baptist Chapels – Vol 2; Sussex, Hellingly: p.127

[5] *Selina of Sussex 1818-1886*, by Leonard Holder: pp 43-47

Chapter 10

Family experiences

Although father employed a goodly number of farm workers, he continued to ensure we children pulled our weight. We girls worked with mother in the house, but it was also a necessity to employ girls from the village, for shorter or longer periods. Tending the chickens and butter-making in the dairy, were also among our responsibilities. The boys learned farm work from father and by their late teens, were asked to think seriously whether they wanted to specialise in this or have training in other trades. It was assumed we girls would one day marry and have homes of our own to run, so it was never suggested we should have any other training other than in the art of homemaking and rearing of children. With new babies arriving nearly every year, we had plenty of practice in the everyday care of infants. Mum's last child, my brother Napthali, arrived on the 20th December, shortly before Christmas 1862, when I was twenty-one.

There was very little time for leisure, but one of the advantages of winter was the dark evenings. The light summer evenings seemed to pass that quickly as there was always plenty to catch up with outside, after our five o'clock high tea. Weeding our kitchen garden, picking soft fruit, (which all seemed to come at once and needed bottling or making into jam), were things I enjoyed but they all consumed considerable time. In the winter however, the dark evenings forced us indoors and gave opportunity to sit around the log fire under the glow of the lamp and have other pastimes. Of course there was always sewing and mending to do and mother would also expect us older girls to amuse the younger ones until they went to bed.

My favourite hobby was pressing wild flowers and sticking them onto sheets of paper which I then sewed together into a book. I would pick any new flowers I found during the spring and summer, put them between two sheets of paper and then place them between the pages of an old heavy Bible. On winter evenings or sometimes on rainy days, as time allowed, I would then stick the pressed flower with at least one of its leaves, on a sheet of paper and write beside it the name and where I'd found it. Some flowers pressed better than others. For the bulkier blossoms, I would hang them up to dry, (or some years I covered them in dry sand), but they were more difficult to bind into a book so I simply kept them on single sheets of paper.

We were pretty isolated from society in general and I later realised how naive I actually was, even into my twenties.

During the summer of 1862, Richard brought home a girlfriend. It came as a shock. Somehow, I still considered him to be a little boy. Elizabeth, or Bessie as we soon began to call her, was only a little older than I was; I found I could relate easily to her. Richard's courtship was exactly as I was conditioned to feel it should be. Their lives were busy. Richard was working on our farm and Bessie was a teacher in the National School near her home in East Chillington, so it was difficult for them to spend time together, but when they did, it was mostly in situations where they could be chaperoned. They were married in the summer of 1863 and lived with us for a few months before they were able to have a farm of their own in Edburton.

With my brother John things were different. John had left home to do an apprenticeship with a butcher in Brighton. He was able to live with his boss and family but became attracted to one of the servant maids in the household, Mary-Ann Blake, (who originally came from the New Forest in Hampshire). One Sunday when visiting us for the day, he mentioned he had a girlfriend and very soon it came out that she was pregnant. [6] I was really shocked. I had no understanding of how John and Mary-Ann could have sinned thus. It was some time later, after my own marriage, I was able to talk to John about it.

'Ruth,' explained John, 'the problem for Mary-Ann and myself was our boss and his wife noticed we were getting over friendly and forbade us to spend time together whilst under their roof. I had to talk to Mary-Ann about this as I could see she was getting depressed. Mary-Ann had missed out on a happy family life. Her father had died when she was quite young, so her mother and family had been forced to leave their tithed cottage in the New Forest. Mary-Ann was the youngest child in the family, therefore in some ways, suffered most from the loss of her father. At the tender age of twelve, she became a housemaid living away from her mother. The various experiences she went through left her with very little self-confidence and a strong tendency towards depression.'

'But John,' I interrupted, 'she allowed you, a man, into her bedroom at night. I couldn't imagine ever doing that before I was married. And you took advantage of her weakness.'

'Yes, I know it sounds bad, but really Ruth it didn't seem like that at the time,' answered my brother. 'I could see Mary-Ann was suffering, I wanted to comfort her and tell her I loved her and wouldn't let her down. The only way was to visit her at night and then as she began to depend on my visits and support, we eventually found ourselves sleeping together. I certainly never considered I was taking advantage of her, foolishly, I saw it as the way to help her.'

Knowing John as I did, I really believe that his intentions were honourable. Sadly, having a child born out of wedlock is not the happiest way to begin married life and as mother tells in her writings, once the couple along with little Emily, came to live in Edburton, Mary-Ann needed a lot of support from us all, but even that failed to save the marriage and a family life for John.

---

[6] *Selina of Sussex 1818-1886*, by Leonard Holder: pp 228-229

Chapter 11

Mr John Grace

I f you asked me to name the one person who had the greatest influence on my early life, apart from my own parents of course, I think I would say Mr John Grace of Brighton.

John Grace[7]

I first remember meeting Mr Grace when we were still at Limden Farm. He was preaching in the Ticehurst area and father invited him to stay with us overnight. He talked with my parents over the supper table and it was one of those occasions when such adult conversation so impressed me that when supper was over and prayers had been said, I continued to sit waiting to hear more, rather than slipping quietly away as my brothers had done.

Much of what was said was beyond me. People, places and events were mentioned, of which I knew nothing, but as Mr Grace talked about his life and his experiences of God, I felt a wonderful warm feeling within, which drew me to him.

---

[7] **Picture:** *Recollections of John Grace:* London 1893 - Frontispiece

Mr Grace was born in Eastbourne in the year 1800. That was an easy date for me to remember. His father, he said, had been a successful businessman but had no time for religion of any form and denied the very existence of God. Things were different with his mother. She been converted soon after her marriage and loved the fellowship of other Christian believers and hearing the gospel preached. This so aggravated her husband, he would sometimes lock her in the bedroom so she couldn't go out.

I remember my reaction to this: I was absolutely horrified and determined before I married, I would make sure my husband-to-be loved Jesus.

Mr Grace went on to say he owed so much to the prayers of his godly mother. 'She once told me' he said, 'several years before I had any true wish to be a practising Christian, she believed God had shown her he had a gracious purpose for my life. He would not only effectively call me to be a committed follower of Jesus, but also make me a preacher of the Gospel.'

Then Mr Grace shared with us different ways God had spoken to him and providentially guided and overruled the circumstances of his life. I was captivated.

'The first time I believe God spoke to me, was when I was just nine years old,' he said, and then with a smile looked across at me and added, 'how old are you my dear?' I was so embarrassed at being brought suddenly into this adult conversation that I became tongue-tied and mother answered for me.

'Ruth was ten on her last birthday,' she said.

'So when still younger than Ruth is now' Mr Grace continued, 'the Bible text *"Ye must be born again"* came suddenly and vividly into my mind. I was playing with orange peel at the time, trying to make a pair of scales. I really had no idea what the words meant but they stayed with me'.

'When I was seventeen my sister, who I really loved and who I could say was my best friend, suddenly died. It was a terrible shock, but as I stood by her lifeless body almost overwhelmed with grief, the fearful thought came to me, *What if this were me and I were to be called suddenly to face my Maker?'*

'At the age of sixteen my father had sent me to Brighton as an apprentice to a Mr Hannington who had a draper's business in North Street. On Sundays, my master and his family attended Providence Chapel in Church Street and insisted on taking me, his young apprentice, with him. I was with Mr Hannington until my father died, when I was eighteen and it was in Providence Chapel, Brighton, through the preaching of Mr Vinall, I began to be convicted of my sinful nature and my need of a Saviour. I longed to know God had forgiven me and searched and prayed for several years for some form of experience that would give me this comfort.'

'I was twenty-one when I married my dear wife, Mary Ades and she had already found the joy of knowing Jesus. My deliverance came on a Tuesday evening, a year later on March 26th 1822, a date I will never forget. I had been able to get away from my duties in Eastbourne and travel the thirteen miles to the Dicker to hear Mr Vinall preach. His sermon was on Jesus' words: *"I am the way, the truth and the life"*; you might say the penny dropped. God's light shone into my mind and heart and I saw Him no longer as a strict judge, but a loving father. To see God through Jesus is to receive his love and acceptance and this is the Gospel message I now love to preach.

It was in Providence Chapel, at the age of thirty-six John began his preaching ministry. Mr Vinall was first and foremost pastor in Lewes, but on Sunday evenings he would travel down to Brighton and preach to those gathered in Providence Chapel; he would also offer pastoral care. For several years, John Grace preached Sunday mornings and Mr Vinall Sunday evenings.

'I respected Mr Vinall tremendously,' Mr Grace continued, 'and benefitted greatly from his ministry, but there was one theological point on which we differed. I was more than happy to simply accept this different interpretation of Scripture and made a point of making no reference to it in my preaching at Providence Chapel, lest I should offend Mr Vinall. However, after some years, he decided it would be better if my regular preaching there stopped.'

'Can I dare ask what that difference was?' asked my father with obvious interest.

'Of course you may,' responded Mr Grace. 'It's the question of baptism. Mr Vinall as you know is an Independent and doesn't practise believer's baptism by immersion. I on the other hand, soon after my conversion, felt the Scriptures instructing me to own my new faith through baptism in the same way the first-century Ethiopian did. You will be familiar with the passage in Acts 8, where we read that after Philip had preached Jesus to the Ethiopian, he asked the apostle, *"what doth hinder me to be baptised?"* And remember Philip's answer and the Ethiopian's confession of faith? *"If thou believest with all thine heart thou mayest."* And he answered and said, *"I believe that Jesus Christ is the Son of God"*. We then read they went down into the water together and Philip baptised him. This Scripture, together with Jesus' command to his disciples at the end of Matthew's Gospel, so convicted me, that I spoke to Mr William Crouch, (who I knew held a baptist persuasion), about my conviction and he baptised me in the pond behind Pell Green farmhouse in Wadhurst. That was in 1832.

Without the commitment of preaching at Providence Chapel, most Sunday mornings, I was of course now free to accept invitations to preach elsewhere. A number of friends from Providence were keen I should preach regularly for them and they began searching for a building in which to meet. As you know, they were able to come to an agreement with the friends worshipping at the Tabernacle Chapel in West Street, Brighton and I began my ministry there on Good Friday 1847. The church there in West Street, had been formed as an Independent cause by Joseph Irons of Camberwell. We continue to welcome both unbaptised and baptised believers to take communion with us, but I'm free to preach believer's baptism as it arises in any Scriptural passage we may be studying.'[8]

After moving to Perching Manor, we attended the ministry of John Grace in Brighton as much as we could, but with father often

---

[8] *Recollections of John Grace:* London 1893

away preaching himself, farm commitments, mum's continuing pregnancies and a large family of young children, it was quite a discipline to travel such a distance to Brighton on a regular basis.

However, John Grace was my favourite preacher and I believe it was essentially through his ministry I was stirred to recognise that an outward form of Christianity was not enough, and I needed a personal experience of Jesus assuring me of his love.

Mr Grace died in March 1865. Mother and Father went to the funeral and I stayed at home to be there for the younger ones. I was tormented in my mind. I longed to have the faith and closeness to Jesus that John Grace had and which came over so clearly in his preaching.

Dicker Chapel celebrating their 100th anniversary in 1913
John Grace was converted here in 1822 and Ruth's
grandfather, Richard Page, was buried here in 1837.

The stark reality of the fact I would never again hear him preach distressed me terribly. Although it seems strange now, I found myself praying that God would let Mr Grace's death be my spiritual life; that I might be able to experience a new life of faith beginning from that date. I beseeched the Lord to let this be. How he answered my prayer I'll recount at a later point.

Chapter 12

The Holders of Albourne

T he village of Albourne lies about five miles north of Perching Manor. It's an extremely pretty village with scattered cottages and farms. A small stream, Cutlers Brook, runs close by the rectory, giving the village its name. Low alder trees line the banks of the stream in places and these, or their earlier ancestors, must have been there for centuries. As generally acknowledged, these trees have given the village the 'Al' part of its name and 'bourne' is an old word for brook. The manor house has links with William Juxon who was Archbishop of Canterbury between 1660 and his death in 1663. Father, who enjoyed history, told us that William Juxon was a Sussex man having been born in Chichester, where he is now buried. He served King Charles I and was chosen to give the king his last rites; he was present at the King's execution. Because he refused to divulge the last words of the king, the story is Cromwell had him imprisoned for a short while and it was following this, he spent time quietly residing at the manor house in Albourne.

There's a triangular village green on the northern side of Albourne around which, amongst the cottages, are a few tradesmen's premises. The village blacksmiths were there, namely, the Holder family. Josiah Holder, who was both a blacksmith and a wheelwright, had a reasonably large business employing about seven men. I understand,

Josiah, who became my father-in-law, had learned the trade from his father William Holder, but I never knew the latter as he died in January 1851 before we moved into this part of Sussex.

We knew the Holder family well as we often met at Providence Chapel, Bolney on a Sunday. It wasn't always possible to travel south to Brighton to attend the ministry of John Grace. Since my parents were friendly with Mr Thomas Blanchard, (not officially pastor, but lived in Bolney and was often preaching there on a Sunday), we frequently attended the smaller Bolney chapel. Father preferred to give business to fellow believers when this was practical, and as their work was of a good standard, we soon got to know the Holder family on a business level also.

I remember sensing that Dan Holder, Josiah's younger son, was often looking across at us as we sat in chapel. By that time, I was already in my early twenties and so, I began to imagine that Dan would make a very respectable and handsome husband for me. However, in those days, it was incredibly difficult for young people of the opposite sex to speak together, alone. In addition, I was the daughter of a respected preacher and also a couple of years older than Dan, all of which created a significant barrier between us. I was rather encouraged in my hopes of a potential husband in Dan, when I saw him appear at the cottage meeting in Henfield, when father was preaching. How I hoped he had come simply because he knew I'd be there with father! However, since I had to leave the meeting before the end to catch the post coach, there was really no opportunity to converse together.

Then circumstances changed and the Holder family moved down to Patcham which meant we no longer saw them in Bolney Chapel. However, Mr John Grace was at that time, still preaching in Brighton, so when my family attended one Sunday, I was thrilled to see the Holder family including Dan, in one of the pews opposite us.

By 1865 I was already twenty-three and very much aware, it was expected of me to find a husband and start a family of my own. I realised, if I wanted Dan Holder, I would have to find a way of indicating to him I was not adverse to his company. Modesty dictated

I couldn't speak more than a few words to him unchaperoned in public, however a smile goes a long way. I decided I would look for the opportunity to visit Dan at work so the best option would be when a horse needed re-shoeing. Wonderfully the chance came one afternoon when I was out visiting someone on Mum's behalf. My horse lost a shoe when I was only about a mile from Patcham. I really think God planned this, as it gave me the best possible reason to call in at the Holder's without arousing suspicion at home. It took me about half an hour to walk my pony into the village of Patcham and remarkably it was Dan there at the anvil, hammering out a piece of metal to repair some form of agricultural machinery. He was quickly able to leave that job and attend to my pony, providing me with a seat as close as was reasonable, so I could watch and we could chat a bit as he worked.

The shoe had been lost, so Dan needed to make and fit a new one. The details of a blacksmith's trade were new to me and I was intrigued to see what was involved in the making of a shoe.

Dan seemed pleased to be able to show me how things were done and to demonstrate his skill. 'You see, Ruth,' he said, 'there are different levels of heat and I need to heat this horse-shoe metal to just the right temperature for me to hammer it into shape.'

'How do you know when it's right?' I asked with interest.

'It's a visual thing,' answered Dan smiling. 'We talk about black heat, dull red heat, bright red and then bright yellow heat, and hottest of all a white heat. The colour is of course the colour of the metal as we see it in the fire.'

Dan had been holding the horse-shoe metal with tongs in the fire as he spoke and his young assistant was blowing the fire with bellows.

'That's how my brother and I learned the trade,' Dan said. 'As boys, Dad showed us how to work the bellows and then as we got stronger, we were allowed to do increasingly more. I remember well the excitement of making my first horse shoe.'

The metal was beginning to look hot. I could see shades of red appearing. 'How hot does it need to be?' I asked innocently.

'In order to hammer it into shape it needs to get shiny red.' Dan answered.

I could feel the increased heat of the fire and moved my stool further away. 'That's wise, Ruth,' said Dan. 'I was about to say you will need to watch out for sparks once I start hammering.'

Dan himself and his young assistant were wearing long leather aprons to protect them from the heat and any sparks that might fly.

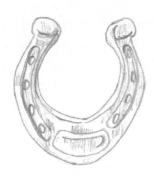

Horse shoe

Soon Dan was hammering the bright red metal into shape, holding it with tongs and hammering onto a large iron anvil. It was lovely to see the metal turning into a horse shoe and I realised it must have taken a lot of practice to get that shape produced so quickly. He needed to put it back into the heat several times as he worked and then when he had it about right he plunged it into a trough of water to cool it and tested it against Dapple's hoof. It needed a bit of adjustment, so back it went into the fire and when it was again hot enough, Dan had it on the anvil under his hammer. It was clear to me that experience played a large part in enabling him to make a shoe of the right size with such expertise; I was duly impressed.

There wasn't much opportunity to talk but I showed myself to be as friendly to Dan as modesty allowed and this seemed to break the ice as soon we were using every opportunity to snatch a few words together. Although it took a few months, Dan eventually asked me to walk out with him. A formal engagement followed and we finally got married at Easter 1868.

I'd like to tell you a bit more about Dan's family, things I learned later when Dan and I could talk more freely. Dan's grandfather, William Holder, had moved to Albourne from Henfield around 1807, taking over the smithy on Albourne Green. Josiah, Dan's father, was born there in 1808. Josiah's first wife, Philadelphia, gave him three children: Elizabeth, Benjamin and Ruth, but she herself died in 1841. After the death of Philadelphia, Josiah married Mary Flint of Bolney in 1842 and Dan was born in 1844.

An interesting fact that Dan used to rather boast about was his link to the Starley family, as his maternal grandmother was a Starley. A

relative, Daniel Starley, was a farmer in Albourne when Dan was a young lad, and his son James became rather famous. Even from a young age in Albourne, James Starley showed an aptitude for inventing new things. This initiative, particularly in regard to new ideas in machinery, somehow gave him the opportunity to move up to London and eventually he became widely known as the 'father of the bicycle industry'. In order to increase speed when propelled by direct drive, James and a partner began to produce bicycles with increasingly larger front wheels and so the 'Penny farthing' was born.

Penny farthing

Also, Dan's brother Benjamin married into this same Starley family in Albourne.

As mentioned already, Josiah Holder was both a wheelwright and a blacksmith. His older son Benjamin specialised in the wheelwright business and when he married, Josiah set him up with his own business in the neighbouring village of Keymer. Dan specialised in the smithy work and when they moved down to Patcham, Josiah made Dan a partner with him in their new business. About the time we got engaged, Josiah formally made over the lease of their premises solely to Dan, simply remaining there to assist and provide advice.

About the same time as the Holder family moved to Patcham, Josiah's daughter Ruth, Dan's half-sister, married James Hills who had a greengrocery business in Patcham. When Ruth's second child William was born, it was very quickly perceived he had a deformity of the spine, which meant he would never be able to walk. I believe this was the main reason why Josiah and Mary Holder decided to retire from the blacksmith's work, to enable them to have time to help out with their crippled grandson. Thus it was after Dan and I married in 1868, we lived over the blacksmith workshop in Patcham and Dan managed his own business. I'll be telling you in due course, more about this little town which became my home for the rest of my life.

Chapter 13

Loved with Everlasting Love

Before I experienced the love of an earthly human husband, I'm thrilled to share with you how I found God's love.

After John Grace died, the concern I had within me to know God as he did, to know Jesus as my Saviour and be assured I was one of the redeemed, grew in momentum. I couldn't speak of this to anyone and because previously I had found excuses as often as possible not to attend chapel services; I tried now to hide my new urgent quest.

I longed to hear God speaking to me, assuring me of his love and yet I felt my own heart to be so cold towards him. The Scripture verse, *'we love him because he first loved us'* tortured me. I'm sure it was the old devil telling me, 'Ruth, you can't love God because he doesn't love you' One of the hymns we sang helped me to see others had come along the same pathway. Its words became my prayer:

O for a glance of heavenly day
To take this stubborn stone away,
And thaw with beams of love divine
This heart, this frozen heart of mine.

But something yet can do the deed,
And that dear something much I need;
Thy Spirit can from dross refine,
And move and melt this heart of mine.

All this went on for some weeks, in fact about three months, until one Sunday, Mr Blanchard preached from a verse in Jeremiah: *'Yea, I have loved thee with an everlasting love therefore with loving kindness have I drawn thee.'*

'My,' I thought to myself. *'This is just the verse I need. Can I really know God is saying this to me?'* During the whole sermon I was longing to feel the preciousness of these words and to sense the witness of God's Spirit with my spirit assuring me God loved me personally.

I went home thoroughly despondent and miserable. What hope was there for me? God might love the whole world but if I didn't know he loved me I was lost.

After a sleepless night, crying to God for his mercy and love and acknowledging my coldness and unworthiness, I had to get up and on with the duties of another day. I had work to do in the dairy and then I took some eggs and milk to a couple of families in Fulking village. I decided to make a detour home across the fields and it was there God wonderfully met with me. Suddenly the verse of Mr Blanchard's sermon came back to my mind and my heart in such a personal and powerful way, I knew beyond any shadow of doubt, God was speaking it to me. I was God's child. I knew it. He loved me with an everlasting love and I could see that all these past spiritual struggles had been drawing me to him and preparing me for this moment. I could believe that Jesus was MY Saviour. He had died for ME and unworthy as I was, I could now trust him to be my shepherd, to guide me through my life and eventually, in his time, bring me to glory. I went home rejoicing. There was no way I could hide it from my dear mother who was working in the kitchen.

Part 3

Married life in Patcham
1868 -1885

Chapter 1

Marriage Union

Dan Holder and I were married on Easter Monday 1868. The service took place in John Grace's chapel, in West Street, Brighton. Although John Grace had been called home to glory in 1865, meaning the chapel had a new minister, Pastor William Harbour, (who incidentally married us), I still thought of the chapel as John Grace's. The Lord blessed our wedding day with lovely spring weather. Since Mother has already given a good account of the occasion, I shall simply mention a few things that were particularly significant to me as I think back now.

Firstly, I was disappointed Father didn't accompany me down the aisle. I believe he had his reasons for this but at the time I felt it most keenly. Thankfully I had two bridesmaids, my sisters Orpha and Naomi but more importantly, there was Dan waiting for me at the front of the chapel.

Secondly, the vows I made publically were very meaningful for me. I knew I was committing myself to Dan Holder for life 'to honour him and obey him till death do us part'. This was rather frightening as I realised he was still in many ways an unknown entity. But then I took great comfort from hearing him promise to love and cherish me and to bestow all his earthly goods upon me. Life was going to be incredibly different, but I was young enough to be excited about the challenge and I knew both Dan and I wanted the Lord to be at the centre of our marriage.

A further important thing for me were the hymns we sang and in particular, the one I chose for us to sing after father had committed us to God at the close of the meal laid on for family and close friends at Perching Manor. I longed for the words of this hymn to be my personal testimony, although I didn't then dare think my faith stretched to the heights it expressed. Singing those beautiful words gave me a wonderful warm feeling inside and the confidence to step forward into my new life as a married woman.

> *Immortal honours rest on Jesus' head;*
> *My God, my portion, and my living bread;*
> *In him I live, upon him cast my care;*
> *He saves from death, destruction, and despair.*
>
> *He is my refuge in each deep distress;*
> *The Lord my strength and glorious righteousness;*
> *Through floods and flames he leads me safely on,*
> *And daily makes his sovereign goodness known.*
>
> *My every need he richly will supply;*
> *Nor will his mercy ever let me die;*
> *In him there dwells a treasure all divine,*
> *And matchless grace has made that treasure mine.*
>
> *O that my soul could love and praise him more,*
> *His beauties trace, his majesty adore;*
> *Live near his heart, upon his bosom lean;*
> *Obey his voice, and all his will esteem.*
>
> *William Gadsby 1773-1844*

Although I was in my twenty-seventh year, (Dan being three years younger than me), I realise now I was very naive and had led quite a sheltered life with my parents and our large family at Perching Manor. Mum however, had tried to prepare me somewhat for marriage.

One evening a week or so before the wedding, she had extracted me from my duties in the house with the suggestion of a breath of fresh air to help clear her head; we walked up the lane towards Edburton church.

'Ruth, I've been wondering what I should say to you from my own experience to help prepare you for marriage. Most of the intimate things I'm afraid you will have to simply experience and work out for yourself as it would be wrong for me to divulge how things were and are in regard to your father and me. What I will say is men can get far more excited and impatient in regard to the physical side of marriage which can be quite overwhelming for us wives at times. But do remember, as you will be reminded in your wedding service, marriage is an ordinance ordained by God and the union between a man and woman is described in the Scriptures as a mystery, revealing something of the union between Christ and his believing people, his church.

What I do want to say is really by way of a bit of advice in helping you to understand Dan and to build a helpful relationship with him. Through living with your brothers you will have already realised how different men are to women. There are not just physical differences, they think and react to things differently. You may sometimes be tempted to feel because Dan is a strong, muscular blacksmith, confident in his trade, all he expects from you is to cook, satisfy his physical needs and provide him with children. Whatever you do, don't be satisfied with simply this role. A true wife is far more and you need to foster a deep friendship together. I've come to see over the years beneath their sometimes brash exterior most men are actually very sensitive and uncertain in relationships and family matters. So you will almost certainly have a vital role to play in nurturing your relationship with Dan to keep the marriage on a firm foundation.'

Mum glanced across to me with a slightly nervous smile and I realised it wasn't easy for her to talk to me in this way. I smiled back encouragingly and waited for her to continue

'You will need to coax Dan into honestly sharing himself with you, Ruth,' she said. 'Many wives never seem to manage this and it needs patience and understanding as he's probably never divulged his innermost thoughts and feelings with anyone and maybe never even analysed them himself. Remember also although the husband is the head of the house you will be the mistress of it. Don't accept without question all he says. I'm not saying you should argue with him, for his male pride may well entrench him deeper in his views, but find ways to gently make suggestions from a woman's point of view. You will probably find he will begin to value your thoughts and opinions and will look to you increasingly for your support and advice. God created us women to be helpmeets for our husbands and that doesn't just mean working for them. I don't believe a man can be a complete person without a wife who has influenced his thinking and given him another dimension to his understanding of humanity. We women too, begin to see things differently when we've had to share ourselves with a husband and produced his children. I've come to realise when God made mankind as male and female, the two are rather like two pieces of a jigsaw and it's only when they can rightly complement each other we get the completeness God intended.

This advice from Mum gave me a whole new concept of marriage. It was so unexpected that the only response I was able to give was to quietly thank her, expressing the hope I could come to her if I needed guidance and help in being a good wife and managing my new home.

Chapter 2

Patcham

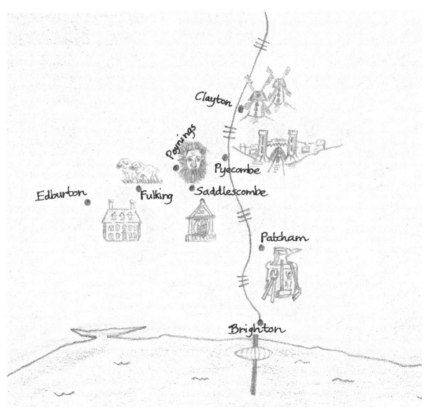

Map

Dan and I made our home in Patcham, a village about ten miles from Perching on the outskirts of Brighton. A few years earlier, Dan's father Josiah had moved his blacksmith's and wheelwright business from Albourne to a new location on the London Road which runs through the centre of this pretty little village. His intention was for Dan to take over the business once he was married, as this would give Josiah and his wife Mary more time to spend with their daughter Ruth. She had settled with her husband in Patcham and given birth to a little son who unfortunately had a severe spinal deformity and demanded constant care and nursing. The property which they had leased comprised the blacksmith's workshop, house and two neighbouring cottages. Prior to our marriage, my father–in–law had transferred the ownership of the lease to Dan less one of the cottages which he retained for himself and his wife.

I have learned more about Patcham over the years and felt increasingly at home there. A major adjustment for me was getting used to the relentless hustle and bustle of village life all around me, as opposed to the quietness of Perching Manor where essentially, all noise and activity stemmed from our own family and farm life. But then, as I had to convince myself in those early months, a blacksmith needs business and therefore must be conveniently located to attract such business.

On the evening of our wedding, Albert, one of our farm workers at Perching Manor, (who had been acting as a driver for the wedding procession), drove Dan and me to our new home. Forge House, adjacent to the blacksmith's workshop was in London Road almost opposite Ladies' Mile Road. It had been Dan's home for some time and he had done a good job in preparing it for me.

'My darling Ruth,' said Dan beaming at me as he lifted me from the trap and carried me over the threshold, 'welcome to your new home.'

As the eldest daughter, I had been used to running a home together with mother but this was quite different. This was my own home and I was mistress of it. I very quickly made various changes to the way Dan had been used to keeping it, although in reality, he had only half lived there. Most days he had eaten with his parents in their neighbouring cottage, naturally his mother had looked after all the cooking and also kept Forge House clean and tidy for him.

My new life with Dan soon settled into a regular pattern. Dan was busy in his blacksmith workshop each day. The business was now well established and he was employing men to assist him. I recollect completing a census form in early 1871 where we entered four blacksmith employees and one young girl, Eliza Newman, living in as housemaid for me. By that time one apprentice blacksmith, John Haynes, was also living with us in Forge House.

My help in the house only came after our children began to arrive, so those early days of our marriage gave me time to organise myself and get things exactly as I wanted. There always seemed to be plenty to do. We were up early and as was the daily routine at Perching Manor, mornings were the time for housework. I very quickly cultivated a section of the garden for growing vegetables and Dan built me a hen house where we accommodated up to a dozen hens and a fine cockerel. Our main meal of the day was at 12.00 noon and this had to be prepared. After midday dinner had been cleared away and washed up, I would change into my afternoon clothes and act more like a lady. If I had caught up with all the necessary household sewing and mending I enjoyed embroidery and this was also the time I could devote to writing.

Dan had earlier applied and been accepted as a special police constable in Patcham, so normally two evenings a week his responsibilities included either attending meetings or patrolling the streets of our town. He could also be called out for additional duties as required. His father Josiah had served in a similar way in Albourne, so a calling to this form of police work seemed to run in the family.

We soon got to know other relatives in Patcham. My father's older sister Ruth

Ballard's Windmill

had married Richard Ballard who as a miller, after the death of his father, had taken over the running of the Patcham windmill, known locally as the Ballard Windmill. My Aunt Ruth had produced seven children for Richard before her tragic, premature death in 1855, the year before our family had moved to Perching. Richard Ballard then remarried a very agreeable lady Frances Willard, whom I understand he had known from childhood. Frances became a good mother to her step-children and also gave Richard three further children. Very sadly she had a serious accident prior to Dan and I settling in Patcham which had left her blind. Once I had settled into my new home, I called to see her and was pleased to note that my cousin Julia, Frances' stepdaughter, was running the household most efficiently.

Chapter 3

Sundays and Brighton

O n Sundays we attended the chapel in Brighton where we
had been married. We were far closer to Brighton than
Perching Manor was and unless hindered by ill health, we
made our way to the Tabernacle each Sunday. We soon discovered the
easiest way of getting down to Brighton was by train. The walk to
Preston Park station was about a mile and a half and once we arrived
in Brighton, it was an easy walk down Queens Road into West Street.
When we began attending Galeed Chapel in Gloucester Road we were
even closer to the station, but that's another story.

Country chapels are usually able to provide somewhere suitable
to tether a pony, but it is far more difficult to arrive in the middle of
Brighton with an animal. Train travel was still a novelty when I was
first married so the journeys to and from Brighton at least once each
Sunday, added to the pleasure of the day.

Preston Park station is situated just south of the Clayton tunnel.
This is one of Sussex's major engineering feats of the 19th century and
enables trains to travel through the South Downs from London to
Brighton. It's more than one and a quarter miles long and took three
years to construct being completed in 1841, the year I was born. Dan
took more interest in trains than I did and he used to like telling me
about them during our rides to Brighton.

Clayton tunnel north end,

One day soon after we were married, Dan suggested he'd like to take me for a trip through the tunnel. Being very much a country girl at heart with a love of horses, modern steam travel was still an enigma to me and the thought of travelling under my beloved South Downs in darkness didn't appeal to me at all.

'But it's not dark,' Dan tried to assure me. 'The inside walls are painted white and there is gas lighting at regular intervals.'

Somehow this still failed to convince me. 'But what about the smoke from the engine,' I responded. 'To sit in an open carriage with smoke filling the tunnel won't be too pleasant, and wasn't there a nasty accident a few years ago?'

'Alright my fussy little wife,' said Dan lovingly, 'I see I shall have to be quite honest with you.'

'It's true it can be quite dark. There are gas lights but often the movement of the trains blows out the flames so the railway men are constantly relighting them.' Then looking at me rather slyly Dan added, 'And before you ask I've also wondered whether this could cause escaping gas to fill the tunnel. However, I'm not aware this has been raised as a danger so I guess they must have found a way of avoiding it. In any case there are regular ventilation shafts which have been bored from the hillside above, helping the smoke and foul air to escape.'

The conversation had been taking place on the train as we travelled down to Brighton one Sunday morning so as we were now approaching Brighton station, I suggested we talk about it more another time.

Being unwilling to drop the subject completely, Dan added, 'I'd really love to take you on a ride through the tunnel Ruth. It's an experience not to be missed.'

'We'll talk about it again Dan,' I answered. 'We ought to be getting our minds ready for chapel now.'

Chapter 4

Clayton Tunnel Train Disaster

nother factor that worried me about a train ride through South Downs tunnel was the knowledge there had been a rather nasty accident a few years earlier. I must confess I didn't know the details but at the time it happened it had been the major talking point of the whole county and doubtless far beyond.

'Dan,' I said one evening, 'if you want me to come on that train ride you'll have to reassure me of the safety of travelling into that dark hole.'

'Oh Ruth,' Dan responded, 'there's really no danger. Trains are using the tunnel many times a day without incident. It's the main route up to London.'

'I'm sure that's true,' I answered, 'but there was a really nasty accident when many passengers were killed. Perhaps that could happen again.'

'I'll explain what happened Ruth,' said Dan leaning across the table to me as we finished our meal. 'It actually took place in the summer of 1861. Dad took a great deal of interest in it and followed all the newspaper reports that came out during the inquiry.

The first major factor which led to the crash started in Brighton. An excursion train with 16 carriages from Portsmouth, which was going on to London, was delayed in reaching Brighton by twenty-three minutes. It left Brighton on its way to London at 08.28. The station master was keen to let a second train leave, (it had been scheduled to depart at 08.15), three minutes later at 08.31, this regular excursion train followed the first. A third passenger train had been due to leave at 08.30 and this was then allowed to follow the other two at 08.35.'

'That's pretty close together,' I said, trying to look intelligent. 'Was that why there was the crash?'

'Yes and no.' answered Dan. 'It was against the regulations which state a minimum of five minutes must be allowed between trains leaving Brighton, but there were other factors. As the first train approached the tunnel, it should have automatically triggered a signal warning danger and stop any following train. Safety regulations only permit one train in the tunnel at a time so the signal man would need to be informed by his colleague at the northern end of the tunnel that the train was safely through, before giving the all clear to a following train. For some reason the mechanism failed to switch the signal to danger and it was only as the second train was approaching the tunnel the signalman noticed this. Being too late to change the signal manually, he waved his red flag wildly as the train passed him and entered the tunnel, but he had no idea whether the driver has seen his flag.'

'So it crashed into the first train,' I said, interrupting Dan's story.

'No, that wasn't it,' replied Dan. 'The driver had seen the red flag and stopped his train as soon as he could inside the tunnel. Then, not knowing what to do, he started to back in order to get further instructions from the signalman. Then of course, the third train approached the tunnel. The signalman stopped it at the first signal and telegraphed through to his colleague to ask whether the first train had yet exited the tunnel. He got a positive answer back and not realising that his colleague was referring to the initial train from Portsmouth, allowed the third train to proceed.'

'Oh dear!' I exclaimed.

'Yes,' said Dan, 'Oh dear, oh dear, oh dear. The third train had picked up speed travelling into the tunnel and crashed into the reversing second train.'

'I seem to remember there were several people killed,' I said sadly.'

'Regrettably so,' responded Dan. 'Twenty-three died and a hundred and seventy-three were injured. They said it was the worst railway accident ever in Britain.'

'But really Ruth,' added Dan, 'you don't need to fear a ride through the tunnel these days. Following the accident they've tightened up on all the relevant safety factors and it is years since all this happened, at least eight years ago.'

'I'm so sorry for the signalman involved,' I said after a few minutes silence. 'It must be a terrible thing to have to live with, even though really it wasn't altogether his fault. Do you know who he was, Dan?'

'Yes, actually I do,' answered Dan. 'His name is Henry Killick and he has a son William who is a couple of years younger than me. William also did an apprenticeship as a blacksmith and I knew him slightly when the family lived in Keymer before Henry got this job with the railway. Thankfully for Killick the inquest in Brighton came to the conclusion he wasn't guilty of any offense. The jury however gave a verdict of manslaughter against Charles Legg, the assistant stationmaster of Brighton station, finding him negligent in starting three trains so close together (against the rules of the company). He was committed to trial for manslaughter, but found not guilty.'

'Dan,' I said, looking my husband in the eyes. 'I must say I'm not very keen for one of our rare outings together, to include a train ride through the Clayton tunnel. I'd really rather go riding with you in God's glorious open air across the top of the South Downs.'

Hearing from Dan about the tunnel disaster reminded me of a conversation between my parents at supper one evening a few weeks after it had all happened. Dad made the comment that as the accident had happened on a Sunday, the Lord's Day many Christians were saying the death and injuries were a judgement of God on those transgressing by pursuing their own pleasure on the Sabbath.

'I'm not so sure myself,' Dad had added. 'We don't really know anything about the poor people who died and to condemn them in this way hardly seems just when millions of others have little or no thought for God; indeed, we ourselves must be offending God's holiness constantly.'

'It's very interesting you should say that,' my mother had replied. 'The sermon by Mr Spurgeon[1] that came through the post this week makes the same point. He was preaching from a verse in Luke's Gospel where Jesus was commenting on accidents that had happened in his day. Jesus actually said, *"Do you think that those who died were worse sinners than others in Israel? I tell you no. Unless you repent you will all likewise perish."'*

'Yes,' answered father, 'I preached on that passage some months ago. I'm quite convinced when Jesus used the word *perish* he was looking beyond physical death to the final judgement. He was warning his hearers and us too, because accidents and death can come so suddenly we need to be ready. Repentance towards God and faith in Jesus Christ are essential to save us from what is intended by that very solemn word *perish*, namely eternal death.'

This conversation had come before I had the assurance of my salvation and I remember going to bed that night, quite troubled.

---

[1] C.H. Spurgeon, sermon No.405 preached 8th September 1861 on Luke 13:1-5

Chapter 5

First Child and Depression

Although we attended chapel regularly, during the first year of my marriage to Dan I grew very lax spiritually. I seemed to lose any strong desire for communion with Jesus and became quite content with nothing deeper than an outward form of Christianity.

Then on 12th March 1869 our first child was born. It wasn't an easy birth. I had a nurse to help me but I was left feeling very weak. The first night after the birth, I heard the nurse complaining she couldn't cope alone and needed help; I think my nerves became even more strained, for I sank into despair and felt desperately ill. Then in a wonderful way, I felt Jesus with me. The Scripture flashed into my mind *'The rain descended, and the floods came, and the winds blew, and beat upon that house; and it fell not: for it was founded upon a rock.'*[2]

'O Rock Christ Jesus, you are so precious!' I said to myself, feeling so confident he was underneath me, supporting me. I recognised what a mercy this was to have the reassurance of his love at my time of deep need, so I knew exactly what name I would give my first baby daughter, Mercy.

---

[2] Matthew 7:25.

During the next few days, this blessedness stayed with me and to reassure me further, the words of a hymn kept going through my head:

"Still, still I am with thee thy troubles to bless,
And sanctify to thee thy deepest distress,"

Little did I know at that point what these troubles would be as I was yet to experience the worst depression of my life?

My nerves, shattered after the trauma of a difficult birth, seemed to affect my mind. Absolutely everything was a worry to me. I could see no hope for my future life, particularly as I feared the contact with my husband would bring about the possibility of another birth. God seemed to be at a distance and the comfort I had experienced faded away as my mind told me it was all a delusion. To be left alone became a torture. Thankfully Dan eventually came to understand something of the way my mind was working and became as sympathetic and helpful as he could.

My mother was extremely supportive during this period of depression, coming to see me as much as she could and kindly sending my sister Mary to be with me and help with baby Mercy. One morning Mum brought me a strange drink. When I asked her what it was, she told me to drink it up first and then she'd tell me about it,

'So Mum, what is it?' I asked, having steadily sipped the hot tea-like concoction until it was cool enough to drink more quickly.

'I called round to see Mrs Robinson at Saddlescombe farm yesterday,' said Mum smiling. 'We talked about your problem and Mrs Robinson commented that they had suffered bouts of depression in her family and had been recommended to make up a tea of St John's Wort which seemed to do the trick.'

St John's Wort

'You know St John's Wort don't you my dear?' Mum added. 'It's a fairly tall plant with yellow flowers. It's not too common on our chalk downs as it prefers a sandy soil, but I found some growing in the hedgerow beside the lane. I'll try and keep you supplied and we'll see whether it helps your mind to think more rationally.'

It was so helpful to have had my sister Mary with me during those difficult weeks. Whether the St John's Wort made any difference I don't know but although I couldn't feel the presence of the Lord, I realised more than ever before how dependant I was upon him and his promise *'My grace is sufficient for Thee'* [3] gave me hope.

Also I kept coming back to those words I believe God gave me, clinging on to them as best I could with my poor troubled mind.

"Still, still I am with thee thy troubles to bless,
And sanctify to thee thy deepest distress,"

Some days I could believe good would come out of my distress and on other days I seemed to lose all hope.

Thankfully by about June, I was feeling rather more like my old self and Mum suggested I should come to Perching for a while. This meant leaving Dan, but with his parents nearby to give him meals, he agreed it would be good for me to get away.

There's a rather interesting incident in regard to my journey to Edburton. My mother had arranged for Albert, one of the farm workers, to drive the pony and trap across to Patcham to pick me up together with Mary and baby Mercy. When Albert arrived, I offered him a pint of light ale which has very low alcohol content so quite harmless. In my befuddled mind however, I poured him a pint of home-made quince wine which was in a similar bottle. Albert must have noticed the difference but he said nothing and slowly drank the whole pint while I was getting us all ready. During the journey I began to notice how erratically he was driving and on a couple of bends we almost ended up in the ditch. Thankfully we reached Perching Manor

---

[3] 2 Corinthians 12:2

safely which I'm sure was God's kindness. You never quite know the alcohol content of home-made wines but it can be quite high and being aware of this, we generally just use a small wine glass and drink it on special occasions. It was several hours before Albert was fit to work again. I believe my father blamed Albert for not commenting on the drink I had given him, but I guess he thought: *'Why she's the boss' daughter and one shouldn't look a gift horse in the mouth.'*

Chapter 6

Experiences Whilst Back Home in Perching

I t was so good to be back in my childhood home. It was now early summer and to waken each morning to the sound of bird song and the familiar farmyard noises echoing through my open bedroom window, brought me a wonderful sense of peace. House martins were nesting under the eaves above my window and from my bed I could see the parent birds swooping up to the nest bringing flies, caught on the wing, to feed their youngsters.

But my nerves were still somewhat frayed and I remember one early morning, I was very tempted to jump out of bed and throw one of my slippers at a row of young swallows perched along the guttering near my window. The parent birds had nested in one of our barns and the young having just learned to fly, had arranged themselves along the edge of the roof twittering wildly to welcome a new day and shouting for their breakfast. Having just fed Mercy and settled her back to sleep in her little crib beside my bed, I myself felt the need to sleep but at four in the morning, as much as I loved birds, this was really too much.

My mother kindly recognised this time as a period of convalescence for me so I could concentrate on regaining my strength and peace of mind and feeding my baby. Other things disturbed me besides the early morning visitors on my roof. As I lay in bed one night thinking about past years, a little voice in my brain suddenly said, '*you were very unkind to your grandma weren't you? Maybe God is punishing you for your sins?*'

My mother's mother had lived with us during the last years of her life and I know I hadn't appreciated her as I should have done. There were certainly times when I was most impatient with her slowness, and latterly as her hearing began to go, I would say quite nasty things behind her back.

I bowed my head in thought and prayer. Then in genuine sorrow, 'Lord,' I said, 'I confess I was sometimes unkind to Grandma. I know I have no excuse but truly I didn't mean her any harm. Please forgive me.'

I then had one of the most wonderful experiences of my life. As I lay there in bed in anguish of mind and spirit for what seemed to me to be hours, suddenly the Lord Jesus appeared to me. I'm not saying it was a physical appearance because it wasn't. I didn't see Jesus with my natural eyes but somehow the vision was just as tangible as a physical appearance, if not more so. I saw him bowed down with grief as he went to the cross bearing my sin. Tears came to my eyes. I knew then all was forgiven. My Saviour had died for me and I loved him. Various Bible verses came to my mind and the meaning of them was wonderfully enforced through what I had seen. One such was from 1 Peter 3:18, I looked it up and found it later: '*For Christ also hath once suffered for sins, the just for the unjust, that he might bring us to God.*' My Jesus was the just one, holy and sinless, I was the sinner who had failed so often to live as I knew I should, but he in love, had suffered and died in my place that he might bring me to God. Oh the joy of knowing this and feeling it too!

However, to my shame, my weak faith didn't manage to hold on long to the blessed assurance I had experienced that evening. The very next day something happened which really frightened me and my reaction is an indication of just how low I was at that time. I had been in my room resting but when I tried to leave the room I discovered the door was locked. I was unable to think about this logically and panicked. I had no faith to believe God was caring for me. My imagination went wild and I began to fear the devil would take me body and soul before anyone could rescue me.

By the time my mother came to find me I was in a real state, trembling all over and it took some time before I regained a reasonable composure. I later discovered that the catch was somewhat faulty and probably it was I myself who had dislodged it when I had shut it tight. It needed the key which I didn't have to unlock it.

My brother Richard was farming further up the lane from Perching at Edburton and whilst staying with my parents, I would occasionally walk up to see my sister-in-law Bessie. We had a good relationship and she could understand something of the way I was feeling, although I don't believe she ever experienced such a deep and long lasting depression as I was going through.

I remember one visit in particular. It was a beautiful warm, sunny day and as I wandered slowly up the lane, drinking in the fragrance of the freshly mown meadow land, skylarks were soaring heavenward singing their little hearts out and my spirit too was lifted in praise to my Maker.

Bessie was busy, so I left her in the house and wandered out to their kitchen garden and the small orchard beyond. I found a seat in the shade under an old misshapen apple tree and gazed reflectively up the hillside in front of me where the sheep were contentedly grazing. My mind went quite naturally to King David's inspired meditation in Psalm twenty-three: *The Lord is my shepherd I shall not want. He maketh me to lie down in green pastures, he leadeth me beside the still waters. He restoreth my soul.* The words came to me with such sweetness and comfort I was sure God himself was speaking them to me. I sat quietly for a while and then slowly walked back to Perching Manor.

On another day, I walked in the other direction up into the village of Fulking to see my sister Orpah.

Orpha had married my husband Dan's best man who she had become acquainted with during the days spent making arrangements for our wedding. They had now been married for about eight months and were running the village store in Fulking.

'Charles and I have been really concerned that you've been so unwell,' said Orpha as she led me through to the back of their shop and into their cosy living quarters. 'I'd been hoping you'd feel able to call and see us.'

'This blackness that sweeps over me is so illogical,' I said sitting down with baby Mercy on a seat by the window. 'I've really got everything to be thankful for and Mercy is such a good baby.'

'May I hold her?' asked Orpha, reaching down to take Mercy from me.'

'Is there any sign of you having a baby of your own?' I asked my sister sensing her eagerness to nurse Mercy.

I realised immediately by Orpha's reaction that I had touched a raw nerve, so to speak.

'Oh Ruth,' she exclaimed. 'We are trying so hard and nothing is happening. Do you think I could be infertile?'

'I'm sure you have no reason to reach that conclusion, Orpha,' I said. 'You've only been married eight months.'

'Yes, but every month is the same. No sign of a baby. And then I think of Mary-Ann. She must have got pregnant almost the first time John got near her and the babies keep coming. Did you know there is another one on the way and because of her mental state it's the last thing they want? It seems so unfair.'

I talked quietly to Orpha for quite a time and told her I would be praying.

'You know my dear,' I said as I was finally leaving. 'Think about this. Some of the most significant people in the Bible were conceived by mothers who had been barren for years before God answered their prayers. Think about Isaac, Samuel, Samson and John the Baptist.'

Chapter 7

More Blessing

K ing David once said, *'It is good for me that I have been afflicted; that I might learn thy statutes.'* [4] and I have to acknowledge that after a year with very few spiritual thoughts, my depression aroused me to seek the Lord with a real sense of urgency. As I have already recorded, God heard my cries and on several occasions applied verses from his word very forcibly to me for my comfort.

The Sunday after my time with Orpha, knowing my brother Richard intended to motor to Shoreham to hear Mr Vine preach, I asked Bessie if I could go with them. Bessie was doubtful saying that Richard didn't like burdening the horse with four people. However when Sunday came, no objection was raised and after all four of us were settled in the trap Richard commented, 'that's unusual, Blackie normally objects when met with too heavy a load and will rear up instead of standing patiently like he has today.'

I recognised this as God's blessing to enable me to go and this was confirmed when the sermon was so applicable. Mr Vine preached from verse sixteen of Ezekiel thirty-four: *'I will seek that which was lost, and bring again that which was driven away, and will bind up that which*

---

[4] Psalm 119:71

was broken, and will strengthen that which was sick: but I will destroy the fat and the strong; I will feed them with judgment.' The way Mr Vine applied this text to his listeners' circumstances described my own experiences exactly and it was wonderful to have my faith confirmed that God was indeed working in my life. He would bring me out of this depression and lead me on for the duration of my married life with Dan.

Following this we had several days of rain and quite miserable weather which added to my depression. One night after a particularly wet day, I just pleaded with the Lord to send us sunshine again and as I woke the next morning to sun streaming through my window my spirits immediately rose. I jumped out of bed and ran to the window opening it wide. It was still early but the sun was already peeping over the hills and pouring its light on the scene before me. There appeared to be diamonds glistening on every leaf of the trees and the grass around was gleaming with freshness as the moisture of the night reflected the sunbeams of a bright new day. I felt sure there was a Bible verse that described the picture before my eyes. *'I must find it,'* I said to myself. *'If this is God speaking to me I must understand what he is saying.'*

When mother's head appeared around the door to see how I was, I called her in and asked her about the Bible verse I wanted to find.

'Yes,' Mum said, looking thoughtful. 'I know the verse you're thinking about. A few years ago I remember reading one of Spurgeon's weekly sermons on that Scripture which struck me quite forcefully at the time. I believe it was something King David said. I don't believe it's in the Psalms so you could look in Samuel.'

After my mother left I got out my Bible and searched through the two books of Samuel. Eventually I found it, right at the end of 2 Samuel in chapter 24 and verse 4: *'And he shall be as the light of the morning, when the sun riseth, even a morning without clouds; as the tender grass springing out of the earth by clear shining after rain.'*

'That's exactly what I saw out of my window,' I said to myself. *'I wonder what it's referring to.'*

When I saw that David was describing the rule of a righteous king, a surge of joy lifted my spirits and I smiled happily to myself. *'King*

Jesus!' I said to myself. *'He's my Lord so his reign in me should bring such a daily freshness and blessing as described by this wonderful picture.'*

Once I was dressed, I began to put my things together to go back to Patcham. I knew the time had come to return to my husband and my responsibilities as wife and mother in my own home.

Chapter 8

Healing

I t took some weeks for that picture of a morning after the rain to become the experience of my mind and heart.

After returning to Patcham, I continued to struggle with waves of depression. Each day, whenever I could get the flowers, I drank at least one cup of an infusion of St John's-Wort as recommended by mother. I'm not sure that it actually helped much but I think it was reassuring to believe it did. Apart from the possible benefits of drinking this herbal remedy it had the advantage of giving me the motivation to walk out into the countryside around Patcham to search for and pick the flowers. The plants are very easy to identify once you get to recognise them. Mum had given me some interesting information about them which I suppose she had gleaned from her own mother who had been well known for her knowledge of herbal remedies. The plant stands about two to three feet high with bright yellow flowers and small oval-veined leaves. Mum shared two tips for ensuring correct identification. Firstly, hold a leaf up to the light and you will see tiny pin-prick holes or perforations. These small perforations give the plant its Latin name *'Hypericum perforatum'*. Then another trick is to pick a flower or bud and squeeze it between your fingertips. If there is a deep red stain, this is the colour of hypericin, one of the active chemical constituents of the plant. Making

155

the drink is very easy. Six or eight fresh flowers are put in a cup and boiling water added. After four or five minutes strain the flower heads away and the 'tea' is ready to drink. It is, in fact, very pleasant to drink having a slight lemony flavour.

I know my husband tried to be supportive during those weeks of struggling. He had to spend long hours at his work, but since our blacksmith's shop was attached to our living premises, he could come back to me for midday lunch and we also tried to get a few hours together in the evenings. However in talking to him I found my depression extremely difficult to verbalise. It wasn't logical. Blackness and hopelessness would suddenly sweep over my mind making me feel completely incapable of fulfilling my duties as a wife and mother. Although I tried to hide it as much as possible, there were several lunch times when Dan came home to find me in tears. Silly things, with which normally I could easily cope, would overwhelm leaving me trembling and fearful.

Thankfully our daughter Mercy was developing well and to see her smile and hear her chuckle lifted my spirts and warmed my heart. Also, I had a girl to help me in the house and I don't think I could have coped without her. But I want now to tell you about another of the most wonderful days of my life.

The day started much as most days at that time with me fighting for the motivation to get out of bed. Mercy was in general a good sleeper but I had breast fed her as usual at about 5.30 when Dan got up and once she settled back to sleep again I gave myself another half hour or so to relax in the warm before forcing my feet onto the cold floor in order to begin the day's activities. Even whilst lying in bed, all my old fears came back to swamp me. These fears seem so groundless now but at the time they were crippling. To begin with I couldn't decide what to wear. I always did my household washing on a Monday and already had a basketful waiting for the appointed day.

'Perhaps I can wear this dress a bit longer?' I reasoned with myself. 'But my petticoat gets sweaty. Can I possibly wear that another day or two? I can't let too much washing build up as I'm sure it's time I changed the bed linen.'

Although not unusual thoughts for me, that morning they seemed momentous, just as every decision was in my state of mind at the time.

'Oh dear! Time is flying by and I need to get Dan some breakfast, he'll be back in before I know where I am. I ought to have had the fire lit long ago.'

So it went on. I staggered from one job to another fearing my own shadow. At last, leaving Mercy under the care of Sarah, my house maid, I escaped from the house with the excuse of finding some more St John's Wort flowers.

It was a glorious morning and the birds were celebrating the joy of being alive. At first I didn't really hear them. My mind was in such turmoil, however gradually God's wonderful creation began to work wonders in my soul and I began to identify and appreciate the sounds around. I spied a robin perched on a low branch singing its little heart out. It was a beautiful sound. Then as I walked on it was as if a blackbird took centre stage. I couldn't see him but the song was so distinctive I could picture him in his best black suit and brilliant yellow bill. Behind him a number of other birds were adding to the chorus and as they sang together I sensed they were representing the whole of the natural world praising their Creator.

'You have every reason to praise him,' I uttered aloud to the birds with tears in my eyes. *'You must do it because at the moment I can't.'*

Then I looked upward. 'O Lord God,' I said. 'I know you sent your Son to be my Saviour and you have assured me of your interest in my wonderful salvation. Although deep in my heart I'm so thankful, please forgive me Lord for not feeling any praise in my heart at the moment. I envy the birds. They seem to have no worries. My body and mind needs your healing Lord. Please help me.'

I wandered on, trying as best I could to take my mind off myself. I looked up at the sun marvelling as I had done so often, although so far away, its rays were warming my upturned face and as I had been taught, giving energy to all life on earth.

'I can quite understand why in the past, people worshipped the sun as a god,' I said to myself.

But this thought directed me to think about what the Bible showed me about the Lord God I believed in.

'*He's far greater than the sun,*' I thought to myself. '*He made the sun together with the moon and all the stars so he must be able to look after me*'.

My mind went to Bible verses I knew. '*And God said, "Let there be light and there was light".* And then, '*he made the sun as the greater light to rule the day and the moon as the lesser light to rule the night. And he made the stars also.*'

Then follows a verse my father often quoted. '*God said, "Let us make man in our image."*'

Other things I had been taught flooded back into my mind. '*We have a personal God, a three-in-one God, who can refer to himself as 'us'. He has made man and that includes me, in his own image, which means I have a personality, as he has. He has breathed his Spirit into us, enabling us to have a relationship with him in a way no animal or bird can have.*'

My mind wandered through different aspects of these Biblical truths. '*The birds do things instinctively. They sing because it's in their nature to sing. Each species has been programmed to sing in a distinctive way, enabling us to identify them by their song. This probably means they don't sing because they are happy, they sing because they are birds created by God. Their song glorifies God in the same way an artist is glorified through a splendid painting he has completed. But for me it's different. God has given me feelings, an inner soul that has the capability of knowing him and appreciating him. When I sing in praise to God, it is with some understanding of who he is and what he has done for me. Then I remembered Jesus had said true worshippers worship the Father in spirit and in truth!*'

'Oh Lord,' I prayed, 'please give me a true spirit of worship. I don't feel much like praising you now, but I do so want to.'

I believe my walk, hearing the birds and my meditations helped me considerably. As I got home a Scripture verse came to my mind with clarity. '*Enter into thy closet, and when thou hast shut thy door, pray to thy Father which is in secret and thy father which seeth in secret shall reward thee openly.'*[5]

Dan was still at work, Mercy was asleep and my maid Sarah was busy in the kitchen. I quietly went up to my room, shut the door and got down on my knees beside my bed. Although I expressed but few words I sensed that my heavenly Father who sees in secret was hearing the cries of my heart.

After what was probably about a quarter of an hour I stood up feeling a sense of peace in my heart such as I hadn't felt for weeks. I knew without any doubt God had come to me and touched my mind. I knew I was healed and the reality of this would stay with me. Never again in the years that followed, even though I gave birth to seven more children and had many stressful experiences as you will read, did such a debilitating depression ever return. I often look back to this healing as a wonderful, confirmatory experience of our heavenly Father's love towards me.

All this happened during the summer of 1869.

---

[5] Matthew 6:6

Chapter 9

John Eli

My second child, John Eli, was born on 16th June 1870. It was a fairly easy birth. As a consequence of my depression following the birth of Mercy, I was somewhat concerned about another possible nervous reaction. Thankfully this didn't happen and I felt reprimanded for my lack of faith.

All my children were born at home under the supervision of the village midwife and I was advised to stay in bed after the birth for as long as was practical. Dan expressed great delight at a little son to add to our family and I was pleased to be able to give him a male heir.

However a few weeks after John Eli's birth, I noticed something a little unusual about one of his eyes. I thought it was my imagination at first but when my mother paid her next visit I asked her opinion about it.

'I can see what you mean Ruth,' she said, looking carefully at John. 'There's a little white spot in the centre of his right eye. It may of course be something or nothing.'

'Maybe I should draw attention to it when the nurse calls by next.' I said. 'I think she is due to come sometime next week. Thankfully it doesn't seem to worry John. Hopefully it's nothing to fret about and will just go away as he gets older.'

Unfortunately it didn't go away and eventually the nurse recommended I take John Eli to a doctor who was an eye specialist.

Thankfully Brighton had a hospital for eye patients, 'The Sussex and Brighton Infirmary for Diseases of the Eye', situated at that time in Queens Road. I went full of hope but received little encouragement from the doctor I saw. He diagnosed John's problem as retinoblastoma, which in layman's terms is eye cancer.

'What treatment can you give?' I asked in alarm.

'I'm very sorry Mrs Holder,' he said, looking at me with a seemingly expressionless face. 'All we can do is to keep your son under observation, but the very real danger is the cancer will spread and affect the brain.'

As the weeks and months went by John Eli became very precious to me. I could see he was deteriorating but thankfully he didn't seem to be in much pain. His behaviour simply didn't develop as a normal baby would.

One day as I looked at John, I felt a sudden wave of both love and guilt. John had done nothing to deserve this. It must be my sin which God was punishing.

That same evening my friend Mrs Ballard had invited me to go down to Brighton with her to hear Mr Blanchard preach. I had arranged with Sarah our maid to look after the children and Dan had been happy for me to go. As I left the house this burden of guilt was weighing heavily on my conscience.

It has often amazed me how in diverse ways God prepares us for the blessings he has purposed. This was one of those occasions.

In his sermon, Mr Blanchard dealt with my situation exactly. He began the service by reading the story of the blind man in John's Gospel. You will remember how the disciples had asked Jesus whether it was this man's personal sin or that of his parents which had been the cause of his blindness. What could have been more appropriate for me that evening? Jesus' answer allayed all my fears. *'Neither hath this man sinned, not his parents: but that the works of God should be made manifest in him.'* [6]

I left Brighton that evening with a warm assurance that whatever happened all was well. I felt reassured once again of my own eternal security through Jesus' death for me and also that God's blessing was on my baby son. This deep quiet assurance stayed with me and John Eli died in 1873 at the tender age of two years and nine months.

This is a good opportunity to say a bit about Mr Thomas Blanchard. He and his wife Jemima lived at Bolney and although not pastor, Mr Blanchard preached at Bolney chapel regularly. As Bolney village is within easy reach of Perching, we as a family often attended his preaching. Mr Blanchard was in demand as a minister in many Sussex chapels and he was a good friend of father's. Sadly he died of cancer in December 1874, a comparatively young man being only in his early forties. Father supported the couple during Mr Blanchard's final illness and was asked to conduct the funeral. Leaping forward in time, a year after my mother's death in 1886, my father married Mr Blanchard's widow Jemima, (eleven years his junior). She then became mistress of Perching Manor and was a faithful wife to my father until his death in 1896.

---

[6] John 9:3

Chapter 10

Dan Holder

Soon after Dan and I married, I became concerned about the cough he always appeared to have. He never seemed to be able to get his bronchial tubes clear. True there were periods when this improved but then lo and behold, he'd develop a cold which always went straight to his chest and took weeks to shift.

Mother of course soon noticed Dan's problem and made sure I always had a good supply of honey. Perching Manor had several beehives and during our childhood, honey had always been an important ingredient of our diet. As well as spreading it on bread, we would have it with fruit and also in some of our drinks. When we could get lemons, mother would give us honey with lemon juice in hot water particularly when we had a cold.

'Make sure Dan drinks as much liquid as possible,' Mum advised me, 'and every day a good spoonful of honey. Tell him to enjoy sucking it off the spoon and then to swallow it slowly.'

In the early days of our marriage, Dan would sometimes relax with a pipe when we were sitting together in the evenings; I knew he would often smoke cigarettes at work. As his bronchial troubles increased, he himself, without any criticism from me, realised smoking aggravated his condition and he stopped the habit.

Of course working over a furnace and inhaling not only smoke but often tiny metal fragments didn't help his lungs, but as time went on he was able to avoid much of this physical work. He was already a master blacksmith when we married, which meant he could train apprentices, so he always had several men working under him. I remember when I had to complete the census form of 1871 we had four employees in the workshop.

Before our marriage, Dan had been employed as a parish constable in Patcham as his father had been in Albourne. This not only gave us some extra income but also got him out of the workshop into the open air. In the summer of 1871 at a parish meeting held in the church hall, Dan was promoted to assistant overseer within the parish and awarded an annual salary of £20.

It was the responsibility of the overseers to provide care for the poor of the parish and a so-called poor tax was levied on house holders to provide finance for this.

In 1880, Dan was appointed as one of two assessors whose job it was to assess the level of tax each householder should pay. Dan was made the collector of the poor tax and his income was raised to £30 a year.

Although this kept Dan very busy, it pleased me that he had this parish work as it ensured many hours away from the smoky atmosphere of the blacksmith's workshop which must have been much better for his health.

Sadly Dan's bronchial problems slowly deteriorated. He suffered a lot with his breathing and got to the point where it became near impossible for him to lie down in bed at night. He was gasping for breath and had to try and sleep upright in a chair. On the 25th May 1885 God took my dear husband to be with himself at the age of 41. On his death certificate the cause of death was given as 'chronic emphysema, pulmonary congestion'.

But I've rather jumped ahead of myself and need to fill in many more details of our life together prior to me being left a young widow.

Chapter 11

Children

Before we lost John Eli in 1873, God gave us our second daughter. Grace was born on 8th March 1872. I love the name Grace, as I had come to appreciate more and more the wonder of God's grace to me.

The meaning of the word grace is undeserved favour and I knew there was no acceptable reason why God should bless me other than through grace. Not only had God, our heavenly Father, provided the means by which he could be legally gracious and forgive all our trespasses and sins, but he had opened my eyes to my need of forgiveness and given me the vital faith which trusts in his Son Jesus. The reaction of John Newton to his awareness of the preciousness of Jesus Christ was to pen the words: *'Amazing grace, how sweet the sound that saved a wretch like me, I once was lost but now am found, was blind but now I see'*, and my heart responded to this.

Our third daughter Mary Ruth was born on 24th July 1875. This name also had a special significance for me and I remember a conversation I had with Dan shortly before her birth.

It was one of those comparatively rare evenings when we were sitting together. True, Dan was looking at some business figures but at least he was with me.

'Baby is moving again,' I said, looking across at Dan. I rather hoped he would want to feel it kicking inside me, but all I got was a grunt in my general direction.

However, after a few minutes when he had finished his calculation, Dan came across and sat next to me. I put aside my needlework and looked up at him.

'Well, what shall we name him or her?' Dan asked, smiling at me reassuringly. 'I'd like a boy to have my name,' he added. 'Although if we felt having two Dans in the family would create problems, I suppose it could be his second name.'

'When I was just eight years old I lost a little brother named Ebenezer,' I said, thinking back to that very difficult time in my childhood. 'I felt God comforted me by showing me when Ruth in the Bible lost her husband, God later gave her another husband and a little baby who became part of the family tree leading to Jesus. I felt strongly then, one day God would give me another Ebenezer who would have his special blessing.'

'That's lovely Ruth,' responded my husband. 'Why not call our next little boy Ebenezer Dan and pray he will grow up to be a blessing to many.'

I was so thrilled at this I couldn't speak at first. I looked at Dan with shining eyes and gave him a hug and a kiss.

The thought God could use our children in his kingdom, became very special to me and during the next few weeks my faith was buoyant and I felt really close to God. When one of the sermons we heard referred to Mary's song, often called the Magnificat. I re-read this passage at home and found my heart re-echoing some of Mary's words:

'My soul doth magnify the Lord, and my spirit hath rejoiced in God my Saviour. For he hath regarded the low estate of his handmaiden: for, behold from henceforth all generations shall call me blessed. For he that is mighty hath done great things for me; and holy is his name. And his mercy is on them that fear him from generation to generation.' [7]

---

[7] Luke 1:46-50

It wasn't that I really felt myself as blessed as Mary. I knew she and she alone could be the mother of God's Son. But I felt God's mercy extended to me. I had the same heavenly Father as Mary and he was blessing me too, unworthy though I was. I understood my blessing came through the son Mary bore, and I prayed there and then that I might have a son who would take the blessing on further.

This identification with Mary continued and I read and re-read the Bible passages about her. Then one evening I felt quite strongly the baby I was carrying was a girl rather than a boy and decided if it wasn't Ebenezer this time I would name a baby girl Mary.

Mary it was, and I loved her. She wasn't a strong child and always had some difficulty walking. I carried her a lot, perhaps more than was wise but I just felt she needed this extra attention.

There was one incident in her life which I remember especially. Mary was nine at the time and was ill in bed. But I too was laid up. I had very inflamed legs and it worried me considerably how I couldn't keep going up and down the stairs to care for Mary. As I lay on the couch with my legs up and worried about my little daughter I felt a strong impression that God was saying to me, '*bring her to me.*'

'Oh,' I said, 'Thank you Lord. You can look after her far better than I can.'

I felt such peace and quietness come over me as in a very deliberate way I gave both the physical and spiritual health of my child over to God.

Mary got better from that illness but she struggled a lot with health throughout her whole life. The doctor said she had a weak heart and in the winter of 1897/8 she developed bronchitis very seriously and died on 14th January 1898 when she was just twenty-two years old.

God gave us our son, Ebenezer Dan, two years after Mary's birth on April 3rd 1877.

We had three more children after Ebenezer, or Eb as we soon began to call him.

Selina Leah was born on 10th February 1880, Joseph on 26th January 1882 and Eli on 10th February 1884.

Joseph also was a weak child and died on 27th May 1883.

Although I strongly believe our times are in God's hands and he gives and takes away, I did often wonder why my children were far less healthy than my mother's fourteen. My parents lost baby Ebenezer but the other thirteen of us developed and grew up healthy. I did wonder whether a blacksmith's cottage was more prone to disease than a farmhouse in a country village. But on the other hand, several of my children were never strong, even from birth.

Chapter 12

Events in 1877

I t was during 1877 that God blessed me with my own little Ebenezer, but the year had made a fearful entrance with one of the worst storms I can remember. The wind was atrocious and the rain accompanying it caused considerable flooding even in Patcham.

One evening during that first week of the year Dan came in from the workshop bursting with news.

'Ruth darling!' he exclaimed, even before taking off his coat, 'I know you love Eastbourne, well…on the night of the storm, the pier was washed away.'

My attachment to Eastbourne was essentially because it was the former home of my favourite pastor and preacher John Grace.

'What!' I responded in alarm. 'You're telling me that brand new pier has been destroyed.'

'You're right. It was new, only built five years ago. If they want another pier at Eastbourne it will need to be built higher and more stable. Over its short life it's already been threatened several times by exceptionally powerful seas.'

'Well,' I further remarked, remembering that night, 'I guess the sea must have been very wild over New Year. What do you know about it Dan?'

'I had James Hammond in the forge this afternoon,' answered Dan. 'He has family down in Eastbourne and was celebrating New Year with them. There's been a lot of interest in the new pier and as the storm worsened hundreds of people turned out to watch the sea, anticipating the pier might not withstand it.

'James said he'd never seen the sea like it. The waves seemed to get bigger by the minute and came roaring to the shore striking the pier with enormous force. At times, the wind took hold of the foaming white tips of the waves creating an all-encompassing mist of spray which blotted out the view of anything.

'The pier master and his men were apparently on the pier when it collapsed, seeing to what they might save.'

'They must have known it was dangerous,' I exclaimed in alarm. 'Did any of them drown?'

'No, but almost', said Dan. 'It was apparently a few minutes after midnight, just as 1877 was commencing, there was a terrifying crash and the shore-end of the pier was gone. The crowd watching feared for the lives of the men but miraculously none of them drowned. They clung to twisted railings and by scrambling onto falling floorboards they were pulled to safety.

'One very foolish man nearly lost his life though. Having seen the chance of a quick bit of money he took a terrible risk by trying to retrieve some lead piping. He rushed into the sea repeatedly to grab lengths as they were being swept in by the waves. One wave was too much for him and sweeping him off his feet sucked him back into the foaming cauldron. Several men risked their lives in saving him.'

James told Dan that both the *Eastbourne Herald* and the *Sussex Daily News* reported all this in detail.[8]

'And all this happened at the dead of night just as the church bells were welcoming in the New Year' I said thoughtfully. 'I wonder if Eastbourne will rebuild the pier.'

---

[8] *The Sussex Weather Book, Froglets Publications Ltd 1991 Page 21*

But something else happened in the early part of 1877 which was much closer to home and at the time far more worrying to Dan and me.

A neighbour, who was never very agreeable, had an accident in the village doing considerable damage to a length of wall. Dan happened to witness the incident and having responsibility in the parish, felt duty bound to make the culprit known.

The incident led to a court case as there was considerable expense involved in putting the damage right and the man in question denied his involvement in the issue. Dan was requested to appear in court as an on-the-spot witness of the incident. Because the man knew Dan's statement would have greater weight than his denial, due to Dan's position as a village constable, he began to threaten us.

I remember the evening he came round to Forge House. He was full of threats as to how he would ruin our business if Dan testified against him. This frightened me considerably and drove me to prayer.

Something else was happening to me during this same period; I was being challenged about the need to be baptised. As you will remember we had been brought up as Independents who didn't practise believer's baptism and didn't place a lot of weight on infant baptism either. Hence, I had never been baptised.

By 1877 we were worshipping regularly at Galeed Chapel, which I shall tell you more about in the next chapter. Galeed was a member of the Strict Baptist churches and clearly preached that baptism was a command of our Lord to all believers. It also insisted on baptism as a condition of church membership and allowed only baptised believers to participate in the Lord's Supper which took place once a month.

Because of these factors, I was feeling myself under increasing pressure to obey Jesus' command and the example of New Testament believers, to apply for baptism. However I had been hesitating for many weeks and felt I needed further assurance from the Lord that I should take that major step.

Looking back now I am rather ashamed of the nature of my prayer in regard to our problem with the neighbour in Patcham. I don't now feel one should bargain with God, but at the time I said to God if He allowed all these threats from our neighbour to come to nothing, I would request baptism at Galeed Chapel.

God graciously heard my prayer and I was baptised and subsequently received into the church as a member in October of that year.

But there was another significant event in 1877. Very sadly about two weeks after the birth of Ebenezer Dan on April the third, my sister Orpha died. We really believe she came to a living faith in the Lord Jesus shortly before her death, but nevertheless it was very sad to lose her. Mum has written in considerable detail about this in her journal so I won't repeat it here.[9]

---

[9] *Selina of Sussex, pages 295-301*

Chapter 13

Galeed Chapel, Brighton

During Mr John Grace's pastorate at the Tabernacle in West Street, Brighton, whilst we lived at Perching Manor Farm, as a family, we would drive as often as possible to hear Mr Grace preach.

Although he had himself been baptised, Mr Grace's church embraced both Baptists and Independents and there was no need to have been baptised as a believer before participating in the Lord's Supper. It was the Holy Spirit anointed preaching of Mr John Grace and his loving pastoral manner that held the church together and filled the chapel with about 800 worshippers each Sunday.

After the death of Mr Grace in 1865, there were two candidates for the pastorate, Mr William Harbour and Mr Henry White. In 1867 all seat holders were given opportunity to vote for the pastor of their choice and Mr Harbour had the majority. However, several out of the minority favouring Mr White were dissatisfied with Mr Harbour's ministry and detached themselves from the larger congregation to meet for fellowship and prayer. On the 30th December 1867 the initial breakaway group together with others formally left the West Street church and met in a hired hall. Mr Henry White was invited to preach for them as often as possible. The new fellowship fairly quickly increased in numbers and it was eventually decided to build a new chapel for themselves. They were able to acquire a site in Gloucester Road and the new chapel was opened in October 1868. Mr White was appointed pastor and on the first Sunday in 1869 he commenced his ministry. The new chapel was named Galeed, being the name Jacob gave to a place of witness between himself and Laban his father-in-law after they had amicably agreed to live separately.[10]

Galeed Chapel

Very soon the friends at Galeed formed themselves into a church with a membership of baptised believers abiding by Strict Baptist principles.

Dan and I were married by Mr Harbour at the Tabernacle on Easter Monday 1868 and we continued to attend Mr Harbour's ministry for some time after we had settled in Patcham. However there were several factors which gradually influenced us to change our allegiance to Galeed.

We had friends in both chapels but one of the leading men at Galeed, Daniel Combridge, was a close friend of my parents largely through his butcher's business in Hove. In fact my sister Elizabeth married the nephew of Mr Combridge, John Martin, who took over his uncle's business and changed his name to Combridge in 1875.

But the main reason we began to attend Galeed was my father's change from an Independent to a Strict Baptist position after he became pastor at Mayfield. Father was himself baptised at Mayfield in 1871 and would occasionally preach at a midweek evening service at Galeed during the period they were without a pastor, after the sudden death of Mr White.

---

[10] *Gen 37: 45-50*

I remember one particular Wednesday evening. Dad was due to preach that evening at Galeed and had called in for afternoon tea before I drove him to Preston Park Station, in order to catch the train down to Brighton.

'Ruth my girl,' he said as he munched a large piece of my cherry cake, 'have you and Dan ever considered baptism? I feel I should mention this to you as I'm sadly aware of the fact that during your upbringing, it's a subject we never said much about.'

I looked at my father, said nothing and waited for him to continue.

'We ourselves didn't set you a very good example,' added father. 'Your mother was baptised as a baby in Mr George Gilbert's chapel at Heathfield as was the way our parents thought in those days. Our chapel in Dicker was under the pastoral oversight of Mr John Vinall of Lewes. He also was an Independent and although I don't really know the reason why, I was never baptised as an infant. I suspect this just shows Mr Vinall didn't hold a very strong view on either child or adult baptism. Like myself for many years, he felt because baptism has been often abused he needed to emphasise rather the need for a change of heart through regeneration by God's Spirit and living faith in Jesus Christ as being more crucial.'

'Recently however, Ruth, I've given greater attention to the New Testament teaching on baptism. I believe now it is linked to repentance and faith in Christ and since Jesus gave his disciples the command to baptise converts in the name of the Father, Son and Holy Spirit, neglecting it is to disobey his command.'

'For me personally, baptism has now become a very positive expression of my faith in Christ,' added father emphatically. 'Paul in his letter to the Romans describes it as a symbolic representation of being buried with Christ and then rising again out of the water to a new life. Whilst this is very clear and powerful, it obviously requires a commitment one shouldn't enter into lightly.'

'As I've said before, when I look back now I'm ashamed that I hesitated so long to be baptised and especially that I bargained with God about it. Thankfully he has since assured me of his love and that he is my gracious heavenly Father.'

During the year 1877 I was also becoming increasingly concerned about Dan's health. He seemed never free from bronchial problems and sometimes had difficulty in breathing. I urged him to avoid being in the smithy workshop as much as possible and to spend time in the fresh air whenever there was the chance.

We were following the pattern set by my father of having morning and evening prayers. It was good to be able to pray together about every aspect of our family life and for each of the children, but I had my own personal prayers about Dan's health.

Chapter 14

Ebenezer Dan Holder

E b, as he was better known, was our fifth child. Mercy was already eight, Grace was five and little Mary Ruth was two years old when Eb arrived. Our only other son, Joseph Eli, had already left us for a better place with Jesus four years previously, so I was thrilled and relieved to find Eb to be a happy, healthy little boy.

Right from the start Eb loved the open air. I was able to have a perambulator for my babies, something unknown to our family when I was young. Mum would wheel my brothers and I around the country lanes in a small wooden cart father had made for us. Eb would lie peacefully in his pram in the garden for hours watching the trees move in the breeze above his head. As he got older, his chief amusement was exploring all there was to find in the garden. He learned to identify butterflies, he loved to watch bees collecting honey from the flowers and one day he managed to catch a little frog and came running in to show me.

We had a small chicken run with a varying number of laying hens and a cockerel. I say a varying number of hens as each year we allowed at least one hen to sit on a batch of eggs which served to increase our small flock and at the other end of the avian life cycle, we regularly ate a hen for Sunday lunch. Eb loved the hens and once he was old enough, he made it his job to feed them and collect the eggs. He also

loved to visit Perching Manor and took a real interest in the farm and
every aspect of country life.

As a young teenager he began collecting birds' eggs. His
grandfather, Eli Page, encouraged him in this and I think he was
also inspired by the small collection his Uncle Richard had. As well
as roaming the countryside and South Downs around Perching and
Edburton, Eb knew the country lanes and hillside nearer home around
Patcham, like the back of his hand.

The girls took very little interest in Eb's passion for nature and
since his father was mostly very busy, he got into the habit of reporting
his adventures to me.

I remember the day he came home with a whole batch of light
brown nightingale eggs.

'Oh Eb!' I exclaimed in alarm, which I'm afraid had the effect of
stifling his fervour somewhat. 'Did you really have to take the whole
nest full of eggs?'

I think his excuse was he liked to have at least a small batch
of each egg in his collection and since it was quite rare to find a
nightingale's nest he felt the need to take more than one egg.

As the deed was done, I felt I should show more interest.

'Did you have to climb a tree for them?' I asked.

'No Mum,' Eb answered looking very pleased with himself, 'I
know nightingales nest on the ground so since I'd been hearing
one singing a number of times as I've passed a particular thicket of
blackthorn, I decided to search around the edge of the bushes. I'm
afraid it meant treading down the grass and undergrowth and once I
discovered the nest I realised I'd unfortunately exposed it rather badly
to predators, which was the main reason I took all the eggs. *If anyone
is going to have all these eggs it had better be me,'* I said to myself.'

Another find that Eb was very proud of was a rook's egg. It was
greenish with brown smudgy markings. He explained to me that it's
difficult to get rooks' eggs as they nest at the top of tall trees.

'They also have vicious beaks,' he added, 'and I don't fancy
encountering an angry mother rook if I ever managed to climb their

tree. It would in any case be a very precarious situation trying to balance on those upper branches where the birds normally nest.'

'So how did you manage to get this one?' I asked with genuine interest.

'This was really cheating,' said my naturalist son. 'Uncle Richard was cutting down an old oak tree. He wanted to do it before it got leaves, but rooks nest early so there was already a nest at the top with eggs in. Several of the eggs broke as the tree fell but I managed to get one whole one to blow for my collection.'

When Eb was fourteen, Brighton Corporaton opened to the public, the Booth Museum in Dyke Road. Entry was free and Eb was fascinated by the display of birds, often with their nest and eggs, all arranged in glass cases and set against backgrounds depicting each bird's natural habitat. He went again and again, as often as he could get into Brighton with time to spare.

It's a fascinating museum and I want to tell you more about it in case you have never visited it. [11]

---

[11] Since 1954 it has been illegal in UK to take birds' eggs from nests in the wild.

Chapter 15

Booth Museum of British Birds

T
he history of this museum is remarkable and became widely known, particularly after its founder Edward Thomas Booth died in 1890 and bequeathed it to Brighton Corporation.

Edward Booth was a man of independent means who devoted his life to the study and collection of British birds. He was born the year before my own entrance into the world, in June 1840. As a young man living in Hastings, here in Sussex, he learned the art of taxidermy, namely preparing, stuffing and mounting dead birds with lifelike effect. Although he was sent to Harrow and then Trinity College, Cambridge to study, his obsession for hunting, shooting and stuffing birds took over and he failed to complete his studies.

He gradually developed the ambitious aim of making a collection of every British bird, acquiring their dead bodies, stuffing them and presenting them behind glass offset by scenery depicting their normal habitat. It was an enormous project but Edward Booth had the financial means and the skill to do this.

After his marriage he built his home, Bleak House, in Dyke Road, Brighton and in 1874 he built a museum in its grounds.

Edward Booth had the instincts of a hunter. He was an excellent shot and had a range of different guns suitable for different birds in various locations. He started hunting in the marshes around Rye

and later spent time on the Norfolk Broads and also in the Scottish
Highlands. He paid appropriate people, such as game keepers and
Scottish ghillies, to watch out for specific species of birds and would
then rush off to shoot them. He acquired an extensive knowledge
of British birds, their habitats and movements. He worked steadily
towards his aim of collecting specimens of every bird found in Britain,
both resident and migratory, of which there are over 600. Also he
aimed to include at least one specimen of both male and female in
both summer and winter plumage, (if this changed), as well as
juveniles. It was a mammoth task. When he died, it was noted that he
was only 50 species short of his goal.

It was said that when waiting to hear of the location of the rare
White-tailed Eagle in Scotland, he had the fire in a locomotive
burning to maintain steam for a whole week so he could rush off
without delay as soon as word came through.

Booth published the details of his exploits, together with
information about many of the birds he'd acquired and he employed
an artist to illustrate his 'Rough Notes'. Edward Neale, his artist, based
his illustrations of the birds on those displayed in Booth's museum. [12]

His notes show his dedication to the task, his interest in the birds
he relentlessly pursued and the vast amount of knowledge he acquired
about the natural world as a result.

After his first visit to the museum Eb came home elated.

'Although it's a shame these birds had to die,' he said, 'the display
in Booth's museum enables me so see so many birds that I'd otherwise
never have the chance to.'

'It's so clever,' he added, 'the birds are displayed so as to show their
natural habitat. In some cases their nest is there with eggs in, in other
cases, particularly the ducks and geese, the male and female birds are
there with their young. You must come with me one day Mum, the
entry is free.'

---

[12] 'Rough Notes on birds observed during 25 years shooting and collecting in the
British Isles'. by E.T. Booth - Available on internet

It was certainly fascinating. I went with Eb on a couple of occasions. Several of the birds exhibited are not residents in Britain, for instance Booth has a wallcreeper in his collection, an amazing looking bird, grey with some black markings and bright red wings. I guess this bird must occasionally visit Britain, as Edward Booth claimed all his birds had been shot in the British Isles. It's hardly the polite way to treat a guest bird visiting our island, but seen from another angle, if Edward Booth hadn't got a specimen of it in his collection, most of us would never have the opportunity of seeing this rather splendid rock-climbing bird.

Chapter 16

The Loss of My Husband

In the years 1885 and 1886 I lost two of the most precious people in my life.

On the 25th May 1885 my husband died. During the previous winter, his nasty cough had become irrevocably worse and I remember that on his 41st birthday on 9th January, we both wondered whether this would be his last.

'Dan darling,' I had said, 'do you think this condition of yours will ever improve?'

'The doctor has labelled it chronic emphysema, pulmonary congestion, which really means it's something I've got to learn to live with,' answered my husband and even attempting to speak brought on another coughing fit.

'Have you considered, my dear,' continued Dan as soon as he could talk again, 'how you would carry on if the Lord took me suddenly whilst you are still young.'

I looked at him in concern. I had no wish to answer such a question but knew I must say something.

'I can't deny that I've thought about it,' I said, 'but it would be such a huge thing that I have decided I must simply leave it with the Lord. If he called you home to himself I have felt some assurance he wouldn't leave me comfortless and helpless. The Scriptures have special

words of comfort for widows and the fatherless, but at the moment I
have no idea how I would cope.'

As Dan's health deteriorated further, we took to reading Bible
passages together that spoke of death and what lay beyond.

One fact that encouraged us greatly and led us to think more
positively about death was that the Bible often refers to such as simply
'falling asleep'. Jesus spoke of both Lazarus and Jairus' daughter as
'sleeping' when it was clear they had died and Paul describes death as
'falling asleep' several times in 1 Corinthians 15.

We decided it must just be the body that could be described in
this way, as several Bible passages indicate that for believers in Jesus,
their spirit goes to be with the Lord when they die. Paul speaks of this
as 'far better' and something he could look forward to. Jesus said to
the dying thief who asked him for mercy, *today you will be with me in
paradise*.

'I guess,' said Dan one evening, 'since we believe from that
wonderful passage in first Corinthians chapter fifteen that these
mortal, weak bodies will wake up as glorious bodies when Jesus
returns, then we can logically speak of them as merely sleeping when
they are laid in the grave.'

The Lord very graciously supported me when Dan was eventually
called to his eternal rest. That first night after his death as I lay in bed
and could very well have been overcome by sorrow for myself and fears
for the future, the following lines came forcibly to my mind:

*'How can I sink with such a prop
As holds the world and all things up?'*

The peace of mind this brought me was still there as we laid
my husband to rest in the graveyard behind the parish church, in
Patcham. In fact the whole occasion felt more like a wedding than a
funeral. As I thought about my dear children, I found myself thanking
God it was Dan whom he had taken and not me. Dan had struggled
with his health for some years and I was clearly the fitter one to care
for and bring up our family.

However, I was very much aware it had been Dan who had brought in the money to support us as a family. He had been the master blacksmith, running the business and training apprentices. What would happen now to our business and source of income? I remembered Dan's words to me during those difficult days when we both knew the emphysema was squeezing his very life from him:

'My darling,' he had said, gasping for breath but looking at me with love in his eyes, 'I'm so sorry this is happening but I have every confidence you could continue the business without me.'

'But how Dan?' I had responded tearfully, 'I know nothing about the smithy business.'

'Listen my dear, during the last months as you know, I've been doing increasingly less in the workshop and in the last weeks really nothing physical at all. James has been running things for me and he is very capable. Our customers are coming to us without us advertising and there has been plenty of work. All you will need to do is make sure payments are received and bills are paid. I suggest you be bold, see how it goes, pray about everything constantly and I've every confidence that with God's help, you will manage.'

As I lay in bed alone that night after the funeral, I recognised forcefully that another stage in my life had begun. I was a widow. I was just 44 years old. I had been married 18 years, but now without a husband, I alone had the responsibility of bringing up my six remaining children and running a blacksmith business. Little Eli who was just 15 months was in his cot beside me. He was restless. The day had been traumatic for us all. I took him into bed with me and gave him my breast. As we snuggled down together, I gathered my thoughts into a quiet prayer: 'Lord Jesus, I'm in thy hands. I can't do this alone but I commit everything to thee. You've promised to be a father to the fatherless and a friend of widows. Thank you Lord.'

Amazingly, the next morning I realised having popped Eli back into his cot, we both must have fallen to sleep quite peacefully.

Part4

Widowhood
1885 -1921

Chapter 1

Relatives

Having a large family and the busyness of life being what it is, family get-togethers were rare, so despite the sadness of the occasion, it was comforting to see a goodly number of family members at Dan's funeral.

When we were growing up it was my brother Samuel to whom I related best, so I was delighted he was able to get to Patcham for the occasion.

Samuel and my older brother John had been the first to leave the family home and they both had lodgings in Brighton with their respective employers. To start with, Samuel had developed a keen interest in milling after a visit we'd made with our father to the windmill near us on the South Downs, known locally as 'Jack'. However working as an apprentice miller in Brighton had not fulfilled his expectations and he decided to try his hand at the butchers' trade. I remember the day he'd come home to talk to father about his thoughts. Our father was a strict but very fair man and although he had expressed some exasperation that Samuel hadn't persevered with the apprenticeship he had chosen, he also wanted him to be content in his work and very soon Samuel obtained a new job with a butcher in Croydon.

Father introduced Samuel to Christian friends worshipping at Providence Chapel, West Street, in Croydon and it was there he met

Mary Ann Gates whom he married in 1866. I remember going to the wedding taken by the pastor, Mr Francis Covell.

I had been looking forward to meeting Mr Covell as father used to often talk about him. He had been a tinsmith but apparently had stammered so badly that often his customers had great difficulty in understanding him. He was converted in a wonderful way and the truth he learned as a result of reading his Bible, had made him utterly dissatisfied with the Anglican Church his parents attended. After a while, a few friends would meet in his cottage to pray and one evening Mr Covell felt strongly he should make a few comments on a particular text. Because of his stammer he hesitated but eventually could not keep silent. Miraculously as he spoke the friends realised his stammer had disappeared. It never returned. They eventually built Providence Chapel for him and he became a wonderful pastor. By the time Samuel was attending, the chapel was filled to capacity each Sunday.[1]

Samuel had a friend from Bolney as his best man, who the family knew well, Charles Mitchell. Charles was also Dan's best man at our wedding and shortly afterwards he married my sister Orpha.

We hadn't seen much of each other over the years, but by the time of Dan's funeral Samuel was running his own successful butcher's business in Croydon and already had ten children. His wife Mary Ann wasn't able to leave the family and come to the funeral but Samuel brought his two oldest daughters, Kate and Naomi with him.

I was pleased to see Kate and Naomi getting on well with some of their cousins. Richard and Bessie's family were there and also my sister Naomi's husband William Rufus Wells had managed to escape from his farm in Herstmonceaux, bringing his two oldest boys, Edward and William. Naomi had very sadly died during the birth of her eleventh child at the end of March that same year. The family were obviously still mourning and trying to get their lives together again after the loss of a precious wife and mother. Mum and Dad were supporting them

---

[1] Six Remarkable Ministers, Francis Covell 1808-1879, edited by R.A. Ramsbottom. Strict Baptist Publications

as much as they could and I found it so encouraging that William wanted to identify himself with my loss too.

My sister Orpha had died in 1877 but it was lovely to have the sympathy and support of her husband Charles. After the death of Orpha, he had married a childhood friend Emily and both she and Charles' adopted daughter Kate were with him. Kate was actually my brother John's daughter but as my mother described in her writings, because of the mental health of John's wife Mary-Ann, there appeared no way that she would cope with another baby. She and John agreed for Orpha and Charles to look after Kate almost from the day of her birth. Orpha had been unable to have children of her own and she and Charles loved Kate dearly. I think having her helped him cope after the death of his own wife. Kate had been just seven when Orpha died and when Charles remarried, Emily had taken over the role of mother; all three seemed to be very content together.

Kate was fifteen at the time of Dan's funeral and it was a pleasure to see how well she related to the other two daughters of my brother John, Ellen and Mary, who were then seventeen and thirteen respectively. Mary-Ann's mental health and severe depression had sadly caused the family to split up so Ellen and Mary had for some years been living with mother and father in Perching Manor. I'm pretty certain Kate knew that Ellen and Mary were in fact her sisters and not her cousins, but the whole situation was very difficult. John, their father, was working as assistant butcher to my brother-in-law John Combridge in Brighton and living in their household. He wasn't at the funeral and because of his circumstances I know he found family occasions understandably very difficult to cope with.

Dan's father Josiah had died in 1884, the previous year, but his mother Mary was able to attend the funeral and his stepbrother Benjamin came down from Keymer. Dan had been quite close to his stepsister Ruth. She had married James Hills and living in Patcham meant she and Dan had been able to see each other fairly frequently, as she was often visiting her parents living next door to us in one of the Forge Cottages. Ruth and James had seven children and several of Dan's nephews and nieces were also present at the graveside.

Chapter 2

Selina's dying testimony

D an's death was in May 1885 and by the end of that year all our family realised mother was also getting weaker and probably had very little time to live.

I believe I had been closer to my mother than any of her other children. She had found it difficult voicing her personal spiritual thoughts and experiences to anyone, even her husband. I believe this was the reason she felt compelled to express them in her writing. My father was always so busy and although I know he sometimes talked to mother about his sermons, in general when at home his wife and family knew him better as a businessman farmer than a Baptist minister. I suppose living in the chapel manse would have made a difference, but the church father pastored, was twenty miles away. We knew how much his ministry and pastoral advice was appreciated, but to his family this side of his life, for the most part, was as remote as the town of Mayfield was from Perching Manor Farm.

After I was married, I used to write to mother every week and she would regularly write back. She benefitted a lot from Mr Blanchard's ministry at Bolney and would often share with me the Scriptures he had preached from and the way his sermons had blessed her. Sadly Mr Blanchard had died in 1874 and although after his passing to glory mother would still mention ways she felt the Lord blessing her, I don't think she ever found another minister of the Gospel that suited her so well. She experienced much blessing from the weekly sermons of Charles Spurgeon which came through the post and would sometimes mention this to me, but I know she didn't like appearing too overtly interested in Spurgeon because father was very wary of his theology. Father had become a Strict Baptist and their denominational magazine, the Gospel Standard, criticised Spurgeon's preaching. From his pulpit in the Metropolitan Tabernacle London, Spurgeon would regularly challenge his congregation to repent of sin and believe in Christ. The Gospel Standard saw this as dangerous, believing the implication was sinful human beings had the ability to come to faith without the necessity of the drawing power of the Holy Spirit.

One morning very early in January 1886, a pony and trap arrived at my door sent from Perching Manor with a message to come at once as mother was very ill. My sister Esther was running the household during mother's illness, (being the oldest daughter still at home until her marriage to William Clifton the following year), so I guessed she had sent the message. What amazed me about the timing of this call was the fact that unusually for that hour in the morning, I was ready to go. I was through my household chores, even my washing, at record speed without any awareness I would be needed at Perching and was just looking around to see what else I needed to do when the trap arrived. I recognised God's hand in this and it's wonderfully encouraging to be reminded our heavenly Father is in control of every event of our lives, especially when these events are not things we would have chosen ourselves.

I've already shared with you some of the details surrounding my mother's death so I won't add much more. I spent as much time at Perching as I could during the days after that initial call, and as mother became steadily weaker, we were all being prepared for the inevitable loss. It is often what we witness as a loved one is dying that the reality of their professed faith in Jesus as their Saviour is confirmed to us. I've heard it said that in the eighteenth century the comment was made to John Wesley that his people died well. To know an assurance deep within us that our Saviour, Jesus Christ, has already paid the punishment for all our sins, gives the believer peace as he or she faces death. This was certainly so for mother. All the doubts she sometimes had experienced about the reality of God's love for her disappeared. She was at peace, anticipating the joy of departing to be with her Saviour. This is clearly more than mere hope. It's what the Bible describes as the witness of God's Spirit with our spirit that we are children of God.

Mother knew several of her children struggled with the issue of faith. As she lay dying, she made it clear to me I was to tell all her dear children and grandchildren that she had found the Saviour to be entirely faithful. Indeed, her experiences on her death bed affirmed to her the Bible was absolute truth and through trusting Jesus there is nothing to fear in death.

Her spirit finally forsook her body to be with the Lord on Monday 8th February 1886, leaving her worn-out physical form at peace, ready to be laid to rest in Edburton churchyard.

Chapter 3

Perching Manor without Selina

T
he loss of my husband was hard. I missed him terribly and the weight of sole responsibility for my family and the business was extremely difficult to bear at times. I firmly believe if I hadn't had God with me and the faith to believe, trust and act on the promises he has given us in his word the Bible, I would have collapsed under the burden of it all. Now less than nine months later, I had lost my mother also.

It was really only after her death I fully realised how important mother was to our family. She had been the central figure in our home. At the time of her passing, of the fourteen children she had borne, only my sister Esther and brother Nap were still unmarried and living at Perching. But mother was also providing a home for two of her granddaughters, Ellen Louise and Mary Jane, John's daughters. Other grandchildren would also come and visit for varying lengths of time and there was always a bedroom available for everyone. Her children spent overnight visits, or came for longer stays when circumstances necessitated, (like myself during my depression) allowing for change and recuperation. In those days holidays of more than a day or two away from the duties and responsibilities of work and home were virtually unknown.

Mother also kept us all in touch with each other. Her regular letter writing showed her interest and concern for each of her children. We all knew unless we requested otherwise, what was revealed in our replies, would be shared around the family. Of course all this stopped when Mother was ill and eventually died. Because of the busyness of our lives and the fact we were scattered over a wide area of Sussex and Surrey, our initial efforts to keep in touch with each waned fairly quickly. My father was also quite good at writing, but his letters were less chatty and more spiritual and he didn't tend to pass on family news unless it was very significant.

As would be expected, it was father who missed mother most. Because he was away a lot with his preaching he had depended on mother to keep the household running and to some degree the farm also. After mother's passing, he still had Esther and two very capable granddaughters to keep things running in the house but he was acutely aware that Esther was intending to marry and his granddaughters couldn't be expected to be there indefinitely. One afternoon later the same year, my father called in to see me on his way to a preaching engagement.

'Ruth,' he said as he sat down with a cup of tea, 'I'm thinking of getting another wife. I need either to employ a housekeeper or remarry.'

To be truthful my first reaction was shock. Not so much the idea of Dad remarrying but more the way he had announced it. If I hadn't held my tongue my initial response would have been: *Dad, you can't acquire a new wife in the same way you would buy a cow, or a new tup at the market.* Instead I looked at him questioningly.

I think my father's next words showed he had sensed my surprise although, perhaps not fully appreciating the reason for it.

'I realise I can never replace your mother Ruth,' he said. 'Selina was the wife of my youth, my faithful companion and helpmeet; we spent a lifetime together. As you know, the day we buried your mother in the churchyard at Edburton, the 12th February, was our 48th wedding anniversary. My initial idea was that once Esther leaves home,

I would simply get a housekeeper, but then I had another thought, which I sincerely hope and pray was God-inspired...'

. *'Eli,'* I thought, *'You have a good home, you have a steady income and you have, I trust, sufficient warmth in your heart for another wife. There are godly widows out there struggling to survive, including one you have cared for over the years. How about it?'*

'Are you thinking of Jemima Blanchard?' I asked, knowing how much both of my parents had respected Thomas Blanchard and his wife.

'Yes, my dear,' answered my father. 'Jemima has been a widow since 1874. She was a good wife to Thomas but it's not been easy for her since he died. I've occasionally called in to see her in recent years. She's been living in the village of Clayton just north of here with her youngest son Charles.'

'I seem to remember the Blanchards had at least four sons,' I said, thinking back to the times we used to meet the family at Bolney chapel.

'Yes,' responded my father. 'Charles is the only one still living with his mother and he is now courting Esther, the daughter of Esther Gates who you might also remember from Bolney Chapel. I proposed marriage to Jemima last week. We talked about it in some detail and she says she'll give me an answer when she's thought and prayed about it.'

I didn't think it was my place to reason with my father about his proposal, but I did seriously wonder how Jemima would adapt to my father as a husband and to becoming the 'lady' of Perching Manor.

I was interested to hear that Charles Blanchard was walking out with Esther Gates. It would be good for Esther to have a suitable husband. I'd met her mother, (also named Esther), who was interestingly about my own age, but had been widowed whilst still in her twenties. Her daughter Esther was an only child and after her husband's tragic death, her father Thomas Parker had taken them back into his home.

Father married Jemima Blanchard on 30th March 1887 at Bolney Chapel. My pastor from Galeed Chapel, Brighton, Mr Popham, took the service and I was one of the witnesses.

My sister Esther had married William Clifton a few weeks earlier, which meant that my new stepmother could immediately take over the running of Perching Manor and provide care for my father.

Our contact over the years meant Jemima was not a stranger to us and we found her to be most kind and thoughtful. She was always very welcoming and seemed to appreciate her new husband's children and grandchildren visiting her, but Perching Manor was never quite the same to us after our mother's passing.

Chapter 4

Blacksmith and Wheelwright

D an had been a master blacksmith and the business he had run together with his father Josiah was commonly known as the village smithy. During the last few years of his life, Dan had spent more time on his second job as Assistant Overseer in the parish, leaving the main running of our blacksmith business to his manager and the lads working under him. Until his father's death, a few months before Dan's, Josiah had also kept an eye on the business and been there to give advice. Now I was left with neither Dan nor my father-in-law and no income from Dan's work in the parish. I had six growing children to feed and clothe.

For the first few months, things seemed to be running smoothly. James Hockham and Adolphas Pollard appeared to be managing adequately. James specialised in machinery repairs and the manufacture of metal tools and equipment, whilst Adolphus had trained more as a ferrier so enjoyed dealing with horses, the making and fitting of their metal shoes. I knew however, if at any time things went wrong, as owner of the business (with no partner to share things with), I would be responsible. The men could simply leave and get another job, but I had my family and was dependant on the income from the business. Therefore I kept a close eye on all that happened in the workshop including the sending out and paying of bills. Casual customers who were just passing by and needed a horse shoeing or similar, were expected to pay cash on the spot, but regular customers could have work done and their expenses put 'on the slate'. In the early days, we literally did have a largish slate on which the men marked up the work done. I would then enter this into my book at the end of the day and rub these jobs off the slate. Our customers knew on Fridays I would be available to receive payments. Although some unpaid bills could mount up, particularly with certain customers, I rarely had to seriously chase the money up.

Money however, became quite tight and one day when this had become a major concern, my father suggested the business could easily include wheelwright work.

'But Dad,' I said, rather fearfully, 'neither I nor my men have had any experience of wheel-making.'

'I'm not suggesting you or your present staff undertake it yourselves,' answered my father. 'You'd just need to find a wheelwright and employ him to develop this new side of the business. A wheelwright works with wood and builds the main structure of the wheel, then your blacksmith is on hand to make the outer iron rim and add it to the wheel.'

I took my father's suggestion seriously, prayed about it and on finding peace in my mind about enlarging the business in this way, began to advertise for a wheelwright. Within a few weeks, I found a man who I felt was right for the job and would work comfortably with the other employees. His name was William Wild from Pagham near Chichester and his wife Ann was a Patcham girl.

William was very talkative, proud of his profession and a good worker. I was keen to learn more about the intricacies of his work and he was pleased to explain. He informed me that the word 'wright'

Wheelwright

came from an old English word ('wryhta') meaning 'woodworker'. The wheels started with a wooden hub, called the nave, which William preferred to make from elm wood. Wooden spokes were made mostly from oak and these were driven into the hub. Because elm has an interwoven grain, this prevents the hub splitting as the spokes are hammered into it. The outer rim which William referred to as the felloe, is made from segments, or fellies of ash wood.

When I queried the need of buying so many different types of wood, William was quite emphatic. He'd explained how oak was necessary for the spokes, (being solid and non-flexible), while the outside fellies needed to be more flexible, hence ash wood was required. Apparently this outside wooden rim takes all the jolts and shocks as the wheels move along the bumpy roads and other wood splits far more easily.

I was very happy to learn all this and to keep my men supplied with what they needed.

Fitting the outer metal rim which binds the wooden wheel together was a job for my blacksmith workers to learn. This iron tyre had to be made smaller than the circumference of the completed wooden wheel and then expanded by heating in the fire before being hammered and pulled onto the wheel. They used what they called a devil's claw to pull the tyre onto the wooded fellies. The wheel was then dropped into water to shrink the metal and close it firmly around the wooden joints of the felloe. Heavy duty wheels would need extra fastening using either nails or bolts through the metal tyre into the fellies. If needed, the tyre would be drilled in readiness for the nails or bolts prior to being fitted into the wheel. Bolts were the most secure because as the name suggests, they were bolted through both the metal tyre and the wooden rim. They of course needed to be countersunk into the tyre.

William was skilled at his trade and as there was money to be made on the production of good quality wheels, adding this to our business helped us to survive financially. I think Dan would have been proud of us.

Chapter 5

My father's last years

My father had nine years with his second wife Jemima before the Lord called him home to himself in 1896. During these years he continued to oversee the running of the farm but was also in great demand as a preacher. Each weekend he travelled the twenty odd miles to Mayfield where he preached twice on a Sunday and attended to any pastoral matters. He was frequently invited to take weddings and funerals in the surrounding villages where many small congregations had no pastoral oversight. These chapels were also pleased for him to preach on weekday evenings and he had a regular itinerary which he followed on an annual basis. I know my father was greatly loved by the people to whom he ministered and his chapel in Mayfield attracted so many worshippers that balconies had to be added to accommodate the numbers flocking in. Being a hardy, country farmer my father didn't often succumb to illness and it would've taken a serious health issue to keep him from following his engagements. After his decease, the church at Mayfield made comment that during 26 years as pastor he only missed three Sundays through ill health.

As he got older my father appreciated being chauffeured to his engagements in his pony and trap and some of his grandchildren loved to do this for him. I remember my niece Mercy, my sister Mary's daughter, telling me a story about times when she and her older sister Mary would pick their grandfather up from Mayfield on a Monday afternoon.

'Auntie Ruth,' said Mercy, with a cheeky grin, 'it was great fun.' Mary would drive the trap with Grandad and me sitting behind. Often when we were on particularly bumpy bits of road, Mary would drive as fast as she dared with the aim of trying to knock Grandad's hat off.'

'You naughty girls,' I answered, trying to look as though I disapproved. 'Did you ever manage to dislodge it?'

'Oh yes, often if there was a bit of wind blowing as well as the bumps. Grandad would call out and Mary would look round innocently to see what had happened. I would then jump down and run back to get his hat. Once it fell in a great puddle. Anyway, Grandad would usually give me a penny which I'd later spend on some toffees. Sadly Mary always insisted I share them with her.'

I couldn't help thinking that my father must have mellowed a lot since our childhood. I don't think we would have got away with such a prank without some form of punishment.

Eli Page was highly regarded both as a farmer and a Baptist minister. Through his experiences at Mayfield Chapel and the obvious success of his ministry, many including other ministers, looked to him for counsel and advice. My pastor at Galeed Chapel, Brighton, Mr J.K. Popham, was a young man when he accepted the call of the church. On visiting my father at Perching, he records in his memoirs the advice father gave him: 'Preach Jesus, be sure to preach Jesus.'

Mr Popham records my father asking him to take his funeral when the time came and of course he felt honoured to do this.

On calling in to see me at one point during the autumn of 1895, father mentioned struggling with constipation and abdominal pain. In my concern I dared to question him further as to whether there was bleeding. Although he hesitated to talk about it, he acknowledged he'd been noticing discolouration in his stools.

'Dad,' I said, 'you really must talk to your doctor about this. It's Mr Candle at Henfield isn't it? There could be something seriously wrong.'

'I've realised that, my dear,' answered my father. 'I've talked to the Lord about it and have a good measure of peace. I'm praying to be able to be useful to my heavenly Master for as long as he wants me here below. The verse that came to me is from Psalm seventy-three verse twenty-four. *"Thou shalt guide me with thy counsel, and afterward receive me to glory."'*

A few days later I went up to Perching to talk to Jemima. She really didn't have much more to add about father's condition but assured me she was looking after him as best she could.

'He keeps so busy though,' she said. 'There are not many evenings we can actually sit down together.'

Father was preaching up to a week or so before his death. He was eventually diagnosed with bowel cancer and died on 26th January, 1896.

The funeral in Edburton revealed how much my dear father was esteemed in the locality. The funeral procession, a considerable company, followed the hearse up the lane from Perching Manor. The hearse halted outside the Edburton village school where a short service was held led by Mr Popham. The coffin was allowed to remain in the hearse but very quickly the school hall was crowded to capacity. Mr Popham read a passage from the first epistle to the Corinthians, chapter fifteen and also some verses from Revelation chapter seven. After giving encouragement to the mourning family and friends from these passages of God's word, he gave a short account of my father as he knew him and the service concluded with the hymn:

> *'Ye souls that trust in Christ rejoice,*
> *Your sins are all forgiven.*
> *Let every Christian raise his voice*
> *And sing the joys of heaven.'*

The hearse then proceeded towards the church and eight of my father's farm employees carried the coffin to its final resting place.

As well as a lengthy report of the funeral in the Sussex Daily News of Monday 3rd February, the Brighton Gazette of Thursday February 6th also gave a brief synopsis of the occasion. I kept a copy of both and include an excerpt below:

'Rarely has the little village of Edburton nestling under the Dyke hills presented a more animated or solemn appearance than it did on Saturday, when in the presence of nearly six hundred people the remains of the late Eli Page were laid to rest. Through East Sussex there was scarcely a better known farmer than the owner of Perching Manor Farm, nor a more respected pastor than the occupant of the pulpit of Mayfield Chapel. And the friends he had made in both capacities attended to pay their respects to the deceased gentleman.'

The loss of my father left me with a gaping void and I was surprised how much I felt the loss of both my parents. *'You've been independent of your parents for years,'* I said to myself. *'Why should you feel this sense of emptiness and isolation?'* But I did and the blessed consequence of it was it drove me to God. I found much comfort in the fact that through my faith in the Lord Jesus I had the assurance of God's word that I was still his beloved daughter and I could approach him as my Father in heaven at any time.

Chapter 6

My Father's Will

One morning soon after the funeral, the postman brought me a letter from Elizabeth's husband John Martin Combridge suggesting that a representative for each of Eli's children should meet together at Perching Manor to hear the reading of the will. My father had appointed three executors and trustees to handle his will, two of his sons-in-law, John Combridge my sister Elizabeth's husband and James Peacock (Mary's husband) and thirdly his wife Jemima's eldest son John Blanchard, a corn dealer in Brighton.

Most of the family were represented when the chosen date arrived and although we all had a fair idea of what my father would have decreed in his last will and testament, we were eager nevertheless to know the details.

John Martin, speaking from the head of the kitchen table, so familiar to us all, initiated the proceedings. 'I think it wise,' he said looking very serious, 'that I read the will through first, then explain it in layman's terms and subsequently address any questions.'

My eldest brother Richard had sadly died two years earlier in 1894. His son Walter together with Richard's widow Bessie were successfully running the farm in Edburton. Both John and Samuel had chosen to be butchers rather than farmers. Taking all this into consideration, we anticipated father would have arranged for our youngest brother Nap to take over Perching Manor Farm. This proved to be the case and the will laid out the details of how this was to be. It explained how father had been able to add Nap to the lease of Perching Manor (which is actually crown property), thus ensuring the possibility of Nap taking it over if he chose to do so. The will pointed out however, that there had been no partnership arrangement between Eli and any of his children, so if Nap wanted to take on the farm he would need to buy the machinery and livestock from the estate. It also laid out details of how once a valuation of this was agreed, Nap must pay this sum to the estate within two weeks.

When a final figure for the value of the estate had been arrived at, the sum was to be divided between Eli's widow Jemima and each of his children in equal shares. In the instance of any children not surviving him, Eli stipulated that their share should be divided equally between all their respective offspring.

However, there was a further point which caused some aggravation and argument. Eli's three sons, Richard, John and Samuel had already benefitted financially from their father by way of loans. The will stated that in order to have a share in their father's estate they would need to pay back the amounts they had received in the past. The alternatives were either to keep the loan, seeing it now as share of their deceased father's estate, or to pay it back and receive further money in the same proportion as the rest of Eli's family.

The whole family had to agree Eli was being very fair and not favouring any one child over another, but I could see my brothers were disappointed. Nap had hoped to be able to take over the farm on easier terms and my other brothers had hoped father would overlook the money they had already received from him. However it was soon obvious there were no grounds for disputing the terms of the will. The trustees agreed to give the boys an idea of the size of the estate as soon as it became clear and this would give them the opportunity to calculate whether or not it was to their advantage to repay the money they had received, in order to have a share in the final estate.

Whilst still mourning the loss of my beloved father, it was quite distressing to have to think in this calculating way about the estate he had left behind and I was thrilled when John Martin suggested we should pray together before we parted. We all knew we didn't need to pray for father as we were sure on the testimony of Scripture and the evidence of his faith in the Saviour he was now with the Lord Jesus in glory. But our lives must go on and we all now faced a more uncertain future without the encouragement and support of either parent. Although only two of our number felt able to pray audibly, in an imperceptible yet remarkable way, I felt there was a good spirit of prayer, drawing us closer together.

Chapter 7

My Brother Nap

O ut of all the family, my youngest brother Naphtali was the most colourful character. The only time he was called by his full name was when he was in trouble, otherwise he was simply Nap. I was already in my twenties when Nap was born and being the youngest in the family, as is often the case, both Dad and Mum were far less strict with him.

Nap was only six when I got married and left home so in some ways he was rather an unknown entity as far as I was concerned. In his later teenage years there were various stories about his wayward antics. For instance, my sister Esther spoke of how he would often creep back into the house in the early hours after a night of playing cards with his cousin and friends on the Brighton side of the Downs. He would ride his pony bare-backed and she was sure by the time he came home, it would have been the pitch black over the top of the Dyke and riding straight down the steep incline was nothing but sheer folly. She told me she warned him of the danger of this. 'What if you fell?' she said, trying to reason with him. 'You could get concussed and no one would know where you were.'

He had laughed and commented, 'the pony would come home and if you found him here in the morning without me you'd just have to send the dog out to look for me.'

My son Eb loved his uncle Nap. I think Nap teased him at times but underneath all the bravado, Nap had an extremely kind nature. Eb went up to Perching as often as he could loving to help his uncle with the farm work and to talk about birds, butterflies and flowers for which they had a mutual love.

Nap missed our mother as much if not more than the rest of us as he had still been living at home when she died. I'm sure the loss of mother prompted him to find a suitable wife to look after him. I'm not sure how he met Elizabeth Haddon she is a native of Northamptonshire, but my suspicion is they met for the first time when Nap drove father up there to preach on one occasion. They married in 1890 when Elizabeth was just twenty and Nap twenty-eight and soon began producing children. I was very pleased when they called their first daughter Selina, showing Nap's love and respect for his late mother.

Being keen to take over Perching Manor Farm after father died, Nap was able to fulfil the conditions father had laid down in the will. He had a charismatic personality and was well liked in the village. Somehow, however one always got the impression that for Nap, life was a game rather than something to be tackled in earnest. He loved hunting and once established as 'lord of the manor', Perching quickly became the gathering point for the local hunt.

Nap with Dolly the hen

As I've mentioned, my son Eb liked to visit Perching as often as he could and one day he came home with a strange story about his uncle.

'You'll never guess mum,' he said smiling. 'Uncle Nap has a pet hen. She's a white Sussex called Dolly. She was roaming around the kitchen and living room when I arrived but immediately Uncle Nap came in and sat in his favourite chair, she jumped up on his lap obviously wanting him to stroke her. Auntie Bessie said Dolly regularly lays her egg in Uncle Nap's bed. I didn't know whether to believe it or not, but she said it was true.'

I smiled and commented, 'I wouldn't put anything past your uncle, Eb, but I wouldn't want our chickens running around my kitchen.'

Sadly Nap died a few months before his 50th birthday in September 1912. Although it was sixteen years after the death of my father, I couldn't help comparing the two funerals. For father, it was a deeply spiritual occasion. The crowd flocking into our village that day in 1886 were predominantly friends from a wide range of Sussex chapels, Christian men and women who had been blessed by God through my father's preaching. My brother's funeral was equally impressive but his mourners were made up of sporting and business friends. Nap had been well liked. He was widely known for his charisma and generosity. In the words of the reporter from The Sussex Agricultural Express:

'Mr Nap Page was known for miles around and his many acts of kindness will be recalled for years to come. One man nearing his eightieth year wept because he was too frail to attend the funeral and pay his final respects to his master. Children stood outside their school with sad, wondering faces remembering occasions when Mr Page had been the leading figure in brightening their lives. He was always cheerful and his geniality and wit made him a welcome figure at many a social gathering. With Mr Page in the chair at any gathering of hunting folk and farmers, a pleasant time was assured and he will be greatly missed in these circles.' [2]

Nap's love for fox hunting was the theme of his funeral and as the newspaper quoted above described the scene:

'The ancient sport was given due recognition on this sad occasion. Mr Page's hunter led the mournful cortege carrying his master's riding boots, hunting cap, crop and wreaths from the Masters of the Southdowns Foxhounds, past and present. The funeral procession wending its way along the road at the foot of the hill was a long one. Officers and brethren

---

[2] *Sussex Agricultural Express - Friday 20 September 1912*

of the Loyal Devil's Dyke Lodge of Oddfellows, of which the deceased was a trustee, preceded the hearse. This was followed by an open carriage containing some of the many beautiful floral tributes. Next came the coaches containing the mourning family and relatives and behind them walked the employees and numerous farming and hunting friends. Several hundred people gathered in the church and at the graveside. The service was of a simple nature. The Rev J. J. Priestly (Rector of Edburton and Rural Dean) officiated, assisted by the Rev W. E. A. Young, rector of Pyecombe. At the close of the service, the hymn 'God moves in a mysterious way' was sung. The polished, elm coffin was borne to the grave by four employees, Messrs W. and G. Beard, D Marchant and W. Steele. It bore the inscription: Naphtali Page, died 11th September 1912, aged 49 years.'

The funeral was an eye-opener for me. I had no idea the extent of his involvement in the life of the rural community as the following list of those who were in attendance reveals: Colonel Campion of the Royal Sussex Regiment, representatives from the Brighton Brookside Harriers, The Southdown Hunt, the East Steyning Rural District Council and the Loyal Devil Dyke Lodge of Oddfellows who had led the funeral procession. In addition, there were wreaths from members of the Brighton Cruising Club, the Southdown Prize Band, Poynings and the Wolstonbury habitation of the Primrose League.

I must say the name of the latter caught my attention as I had no idea what sort of club this was and imagined it must have something to do with the preservation of plants. At the first opportunity I asked Nap's widow Bessie if she knew what it was all about. Her answer was something of a let-down:

'No Ruth,' she said smiling, 'the organisation is political and has nothing to do with primroses at all. Nap was a paying member and its aim was to promote conservative political principles.'

'To call it the Primrose League rather hints at wanting to cover up its main objective.' I suggested.

'I'm not sure about that,' said Bessie. 'Nap once explained to me that the primrose was the favourite flower of an important politician. I think it was Disraeli. This was so well known that at his funeral,

Queen Victoria sent a wreath of primroses. I believe Lord Randolph Churchill was a leading figure in the creation of the League.'

After the death of Nap, the Page family lost the tenancy of Perching Manor Farm.

Chapter 8

Concern for my children

A lthough looking back, I can with sincerity praise God for the way he kept our business going, enabling me to pay our employees promptly and giving me sufficient funds to provide for my family, I admit there were some truly testing times. Again and again over the years, I would go back to the Lord to declare him Master, not only of my life but also of my business: 'Lord, clerks do not find the money to pay bills; the Master does.'

After Dan's death, being a single parent made me realise my total dependence on God for the upbringing of my children. I prayed to him about them constantly and sought wisdom to be the best mother possible to each one. Ebenezer Dan was my eldest son and my hope was he would want to be a blacksmith taking over the running of the business. Eb however was a gentle lad, an avid reader and far more interested in study than flexing his muscles in the blacksmith shop. I wanted the best for him and was pleased when he was accepted for the grammar school in Brighton. From there he went on to qualify as a clerk and eventually got a position in London. He married a lovely Christian girl, Mary Gertrude White in 1908 and their first home was in Norwood closer to his place of work. Although Eb didn't make an open confession of his Christian faith in baptism, after his questionable teenage years, I never really had any doubt that his heart was right before God.

Mary was born two years before Eb but was always a great concern to me. She was never strong and died of consumption in 1898 in her twenty-third year. During her last illness I pleaded with the Lord for her but he saw best to take her. She had never spoken of her faith and after she died I was tormented with the thought that she had passed into eternity without trusting the Saviour. This burden stayed with me for a full year. I besought the Lord to assure me of her salvation and waited expectantly for him to speak comfort to me in some way.

During that whole year my mind and spirit went helter-skelter. I could find no lasting peace about Mary nor would my mind let the matter rest. My prayer life was dominated by my concern to know she was safely with the Lord. I knew no prayer of mine could change her destiny, but in my love for her I needed to be sure she was accepted in Jesus and that I would meet her again in glory.

I cried to the Lord to give me a word of assurance through Mr Popham's preaching but several times the Scripture that seemed to speak to me was 'My honour I will not give to another'.

'Now, what does that mean?' I cried to the Lord, bewildered. 'I have no thought that my prayers can make her worthy of heaven. It's all of thy grace. I simply long to have the peace of knowing she is with you.'

Then the thought, no doubt prompted by the enemy, that it would be far worse for me if God showed me Satan had her in his kingdom. *'Better let the whole matter rest and learn to live with an uncertain hope.'* was the temptation.

For a short while I tried to do this, but the thought of my beloved child held captive by Satan for all eternity tormented me beyond endurance. Then God graciously ministered to my soul on three separate occasions giving me hope. The first occurred one evening as I was simply crossing the room, a hymn we used to sing as children came powerfully to my mind.

'Around the throne of God in heaven,
Thousands of children stand,
Children whose sins are all forgiven,
A holy, happy band.'

Tears welled up as I sang quietly to myself.

Another time when praying, I felt so close to the Lord in my crying about Mary it was as if I was actually washing my Saviour's feet with my tears and wiping them with my hair. Oh the blessedness I enjoyed, but when I eventually rose from my knees and got into bed this inner peace slowly faded. I found myself thinking: *'That was nothing more than your own imagination.'*

On the third occasion, I was really challenged and emotionally moved when reading in the Song of Solomon: *'Who is this that cometh up out of the wilderness, leaning upon her Beloved?'*[3] I could do nothing but weep before the Lord. It was as though he was right there with me in the room. I shall never forget the experience. 'Lord,' I cried, 'how can you ever bless me! Look at my rebellion! I know I haven't been leaning on you as I should.'

In a gracious way he showed me how part of me had been leaning on him, yet the rest of me had been in total rebellion. I saw clearly the two natures at odds with one another. My old human nature would have torn him from his throne for the way he was dealing with me in my anguish over Mary, yet all the while there was another new spirit within, submissive and willing to bear all that he saw fit to lay on me. I recognised that there were times when in the words of Job, I could sincerely say: *The Lord has given and the Lord has taken away, blessed be the name of the Lord.*[4] Oh the peace I experienced when this spirit had the upper hand! Sadly these times never lasted long and the old rebellion returned.

'Lord,' I said, 'this trusting spirit within me, although weak at times, is evidence of your grace towards me. Thank you so much.'

---

[3] Song of Solomon 8:5
[4] Job 1:21

As I got into bed, the old tempter returned. *'This still doesn't give you any assurance about Mary,'* said the voice inside my head.

At that moment, the words of a hymn by Joseph Hart came as succour to my soul:

Urge thy claim through all unfitness,
Sue it out, spurning doubt,
The Holy Ghost's thy witness.

I felt I was in the arms of my Saviour and I went peacefully to sleep.

By this stage, the Lord had blessed me with a good measure of reassurance but like a dog with a bone, my poor mind wouldn't let the matter rest. It was a good number of weeks later that something Mr Popham said in the course of his sermon one Sunday morning caused the old devil to say to me: *'There! That has come straight from God through your pastor. Now let her drop, there is no ground to hope.'*

'No,' I shouted back under my breath. 'I refuse to let her go. I won't let the matter drop.'

When I got home I asked Lily if she had ever known Mary to pray.

'Mother,' answered my daughter looking at me strangely. 'What else do you imagine she was doing when she was so often on her knees? We shared a room so I could scarcely miss it.'

Finally through God's grace and mercy I had all the reassurance I needed.

It was the evening of the first Sunday in the month and I was sitting at the Lord's table in Galeed Chapel. Once again I was feeling desperate. I hadn't found lasting peace about Mary and the enemy still kept torturing me with his claims on her.

'How can I keep on going, Lord?' I cried in my silent, desperate prayer.

The Lord answered me and praise to his name, he gave lasting peace to enable me to trust him completely with my daughter.

'She's mine I bought her with my blood.' These words were enough, my heart and mind needed no further persuasion. I took the wine as

it was passed to me and could think of it as the blood of my Saviour both for me and my departed children.

'That will do Lord. It's enough,' I responded, with deepest joy. If you want to take them to heaven, you may take every one.'

Some years later in 1905, that heartfelt response of mine came starkly to my remembrance. My beloved daughter Lily, my pet name for Selina Leah, was dying aged twenty-five years.

It was as if the Lord said to me, 'you said I could take them all.'

My immediate response was, 'yes, Lord, but only on the condition you take them to yourself.'

As I sat with my dying daughter, holding her hand and praying for her, from her peaceful demeanour and the Lord's reassurance, in my heart I knew he was taking her to be with him.

She was unconscious, nevertheless I leaned across gently kissing her forehead and whispered 'goodbye'. Although losing another child brought such sorrow, I sensed the Lord's peace surpassing all understanding, guarding my breaking heart.

Chapter 9

Marriages and Grandchildren

My eldest daughter Mercy Elizabeth was first to marry. The service took place in Galeed Chapel, Brighton on Monday 4th January 1892 when she married Frank Belcher. Their first home was in Westham, east of Eastbourne. Although technically still in Sussex, it was unfortunately too distant for us to meet up often. They began producing grandchildren for me almost immediately and in the October following their marriage, Alfred Holder Belcher was born. At first I found having to share my daughter with another family quite difficult to cope with and having a grandson with the name Alfred (not one of our family names) seemed strange. I associated the name with one of our farm workers at Perching, who was a simple soul, but as Frank's father was called Alfred, once we became better acquainted, I accepted the choice. Giving little Alfred the second name of Holder, naturally pleased me immensely.

Their second child was born in April 1894, my first granddaughter who very happily for me, was named Mary Ruth. By the time their third child Olive Grace was born two years later, the family had moved to Cobham in Surrey, where Frank had his own grocery and drapery business. Mercy gave me seven grandchildren before my son Eb married. For a number of years, Eb had been courting Mary Gertrude White (whom he had met at Galeed Chapel), but he was thirty-one before he finally married in 1908. Gertie, as she was affectionately known, was seven years his junior and the daughter of George White, a blacksmith with a business on the Lewes Road, Brighton. Eb was working as an insurance clerk in the city of London and living at South Norwood when he married and the wedding was a very quiet affair conducted one Sunday morning, 13th September, in his local parish church. My youngest son Eli and I were the only Holder family members to attend, together with Gertie's parents, George and Fanny White.

The White family faithfully attended Galeed Chapel and when Eb and Gertie began to get friendly, Fanny invited me round for afternoon tea so we could get better acquainted. George joined us briefly for a cup of tea and the conversation soon revealed he had been brought up in Berwick close to the Dicker where I had been born. His father had been a blacksmith in Berwick and the family had attended Zoar Chapel, Dicker. George informed me he was the child of his father's second marriage and had six half brothers and sisters from his father's first marriage to Frances Gay Dunk.

'George,' I said with great interest, 'the name Dunk is familiar. My father used to refer to the little Independent Chapel at Lower Dicker, where my grandparents are buried as Dunk's Chapel. Also I'm sure I remember hearing that a Mr Dunk was one of the founding members of the new Dicker Chapel when it was first built.'

'Yes,' answered George smiling, 'the Dunks are well known in the Dicker area as being a prominent nonconformist family and my father's first wife Frances Dunk is buried in the Dicker Chapel burial ground. As I understand it, the chapel in Lower Dicker was built by one of the Dunk family on part of his farmland and I also believe the plot of land on which Zoar Chapel is built, was also purchased for this use by the Dunks.'

The possibility of a family link back to the area of my parents upbringing through the marriage of my son Ebenezer thrilled me, although at that point, I realised it was extremely unlikely, knowing Eb, that he had even asked Gertie for her hand. I could well imagine my quiet son being rather like the Sussex farmer's son, who whilst jogging home with his girl in the pony and trap after an evening out, suddenly burst out, "Will yer 'ave me?" She looked up at him nodding positively. After a quarter of an hour of silence she eventually added, "haven't you got anything else to say?" To which he answered, "I'm wondering if I ain't said too much already."

I was suddenly jolted back to the present on hearing George add, 'another well-known family name which might have meaning for you is that of Funnell.'

'Yes,' I said. 'There is I believe a Thomas Funnell who is pastor of the chapel in the village of Blackboys, just north of the Dicker.'

'That's who I had in mind,' replied George. 'Well Frances Dunk's mother was Elizabeth Funnell, sister I believe to Thomas Funnell's father.'

'Well, well,' I murmured, 'these family connections are quite extraordinary.'

Fanny White had been listening to our conversation with interest and glancing at her husband said, 'Blackboys is such a peculiar name for a village. Do you know the reason why?'

'I've heard said,' answered her husband smiling at his wife, 'the name is due to the soot that regularly blew into the village from the charcoal burning in the surrounding forest.'

As I journeyed home, I thought over what I had heard and experienced of the White family. George had the same profession as my Dan and moreover, had left me with the running of. I rather gathered however, that George specialised more on the shoe-smith side of the trade. I had also discovered that Fanny ran a fruiterer's business with Gertie assisting her. All this, together with their family connections at the Dicker, drew me to the family and I couldn't help hoping that the friendship Eb had with Gertie would result in marriage. Naturally, when that's exactly what happened in 1908, I couldn't have been more pleased.

Chapter 10

Final Years

My youngest child, Eli, learned the smithy business but concentrated on what is known as the work of a whitesmith. I encouraged him in this as it complemented the well-established blacksmith business. Whilst a blacksmith works with the raw metal, softening iron in the furnace and moulding it to make horse-shoes, ploughshares, chains and suchlike, the whitesmith works with smaller more delicate items, for example, locks, keys, and carpenters' tools which require filing and smoothing making use of lighter metals such as tin. Eli has now taken on overall responsibility for the business relieving me considerably. In 1917 Eli married his cousin Ruby Peacock, the daughter of my sister Mary.

Before Eli married, Eb and Gertie had produced three additional grandchildren for me. Edgar Ebenezer [5] was the eldest born in 1909, then Gertrude Mary in 1911 and Ruth in 1913.

I enjoyed visits from my grandchildren but unfortunately I developed the notion that they thought I might be a witch. One problem was my teeth. As was often the case when I was a girl, I had yielded to the recommended procedure of having all my teeth extracted before getting married. The logic being it saved on dentist

---

[5] Edgar Ebenezer was the author's father.

bills later when producing children. Calcium necessary for the development and growth of children in the womb was extracted from the mother's body and this very often caused the teeth to weaken and require expensive treatment. As I got older my gums shrunk somewhat so that my dentures, made for me when I was younger, no longer fitted properly. I know I could have had new ones made but it was easier to simply live toothless and just put my teeth in on Sundays and special occasions. I would explain to my grandchildren that grandma kept the 'dining room furniture' for her mouth upstairs in the drawer by her bed. [6]

None of my grandchildren are being raised on farms as I had so I thought once they were old enough, it would be a good idea to introduce them to some aspects of farming. My chickens gave me the perfect opportunity as the children were often keen to watch me feeding the fowls. On more than one occasion I asked them to help me kill a chicken for dinner. As I got older I found it increasingly difficult to break the chicken's neck with my hands and as it was always my intention to get the deed over as quickly as possible to avoid suffering for the bird, I invented a way of chopping off the creature's head with one foul stroke!

'Pat,' I said, using the pet name for my grandson, Walter Frank, 'I need you to help kill tomorrow's lunch. Are you game?'

'Of course Grandma,' answered Pat, 'tell me what to do.'

'Firstly, when I catch the hen, I hold it under my arm and tie this string around its neck.'

This was quite easily achieved.

'Now my dear, I'll hold the bird down on the table here. See I'm putting some layers of old newspaper on it first to catch the blood. Once I've got the bird pinned down with my left hand and have the axe ready in my right hand, I want you to pull the string taut in order to stretch out the bird's neck. Good that's just fine.'

---

[6] John Richard Thomas, 'Oral history'; A Page in Time. Unpublished family research of the Page family,

I bring the axe down quickly and accurately on the bird's neck and the deed is done.

'Grandma!' exclaimed Pat quite shocked about the whole procedure. 'Look, the chicken is running away without its head!' [7]

I explained to my grandson that although the bird was quite dead, its nervous system was reacting with some sort of reflex causing it to flap across the garden.

I suppose, now I think about it, it's not surprising the children consider me to be an old witch.

During my latter years I often reminisced about the idea I once had that Ebenezer, the son I believe God gave me to replace the little brother taken from us when I was only nine, would be used by God to further His kingdom. I've said nothing of this directly to Eb himself, but pray regularly for him and his children and have watched with great interest the development of his life.

Eb and Gertie's three children were born in Norwood, their first home together. Prior to the final illness of Fanny, Gertie's mother, they moved down to Brighton so Gertie could nurse her and care for her father George. Their Brighton home is now on Stanley Road, the

Patcham side of Brighton, so it is pure joy for me to see more of them and to get to know my grandchildren, Edgar, Gertie and Ruth. Eb travels up to London for his job as a clerk in an insurance office, the Provident Association of London. The train service from Brighton to London is regular and convenient and Dan would have been so proud seeing his son in city attire: a three-piece pinstriped suit and tie, bowler hat and umbrella.

Ebenezer Holder

---

[7] John Richard Thomas, 'Oral history'; A Page in Time. Unpublished family research of the Page family

To have Eb nearer at hand is a great comfort to me particularly after the loss of my beloved daughter Grace in 1917. Grace had never married and had been a dear, loving companion for me. When the Lord called her home to himself on 14h April 1917, I missed her terribly. I had no fears about her eternal destiny. She loved the Lord Jesus and eagerly attended the services at Galeed Chapel confirming her renewed spiritual life. There had been no sign of illness before having a fall on 24th March from which she never recovered, suffering severe pain and also some mental disturbance. Eventually the doctors diagnosed Bright's disease which they described as a disease of the kidneys. Grace was just 45 when she died and is buried near her father in the Patcham grave yard, waiting for the wonderful day of resurrection when our Saviour returns.

Since losing Grace it has become much more evident how difficult it is for me to write. My memory has suddenly begun to let me down. Although I'm able to enjoy seeing my family, collecting eggs from my chickens and on Sundays attending the ministry of Mr Popham in Brighton, when I try to think of what I did yesterday or what anyone said to me I search and search my mind but frustratingly to no avail. A particular verse of a hymn keeps coming to my mind however:

'In every state secure,
Kept as Jehovah's eye,
'Tis well with them while life endure,
And well when call'd to die.'

The Lord gives me great inner peace and I find myself conversing with him most of the day. I know he doesn't mind if I repeat myself and I'm looking forward to seeing him very soon.

Ruth died peacefully on April 20th 1921, aged 79 years. She suffered a cerebral embolism whilst eating her breakfast on the

Sunday morning before her death. After lying unconscious until the Wednesday evening, she mercifully passed from this life without the slightest murmur, gently taken to be with her beloved Saviour for eternity.

Index

Lightning Source UK Ltd.
Milton Keynes UK
UKHW012305190620
365278UK00002B/72